PORSCHE

PORSCHE

MIKE McCARTHY

GALLERY BOOKS
An imprint of W.H. Smith Publishers Inc.
112 Madison Avenue
New York, New York 10016

A Bison Book

Published by Gallery Books
A Division of W H Smith Publishers Inc.
112 Madison Avenue
New York, New York, 10016

Produced by
Bison Books Corp.
17 Sherwood Place
Greenwich, CT 06830

ISBN 0-8317-7088-0

Printed in Hong Kong

1 2 3 4 5 6 7 8 9 10

CONTENTS

THE PORSCHE DYNASTY

'My Other Car's a Porsche' proclaim those bumper stickers you see, invariably on a tattered and rusty heap, and nothing seems to sum up the Porsche mystique quite so accurately, if frivolously. In today's world, a Porsche is not simply a car, it is a symbol of much that many find desirable, a thoroughbred racehorse among ponies.

Just what the founder of the company, the late Ferdinand Anton Porsche, would have made of that sticker is anybody's guess. He might have been wryly amused but more likely would have regarded it as too silly to be worthy of much attention. Yet, I suspect he would have been secretly rather proud because the significance of the name has not come about through any advertising hype or passing fashions but through years of hard graft and dedication to principles he laid down in his lifetime.

It is customary to think of Porsche as a product of the postwar German revival and this is true of the cars. But in fact Porsche, in the person of Ferdinand Anton, has been around in matters automotive almost as long as the automobile itself. He was but 10 years old when the first self-propelled devices of Messrs Daimler and Benz phut-phutted their precarious way into the history books along the roads of southern Germany.

He was born, the third of five children, to a tinsmith, Anton Porsche, in the village of Maffersdorf, in the area traditionally known as Bohemia. At the time of his birth this was part of the Austro-Hungarian Empire but after World War I it was seceded to the new state of Czechoslovakia. It was also part of the Sudetenland, that part of Czechoslovakia which Hitler so deeply desired, so the Porsche family could be called Sudeten Germans. In fact, they have always regarded themselves as Austrians.

Ferdinand's first love was electricity – there is a well-known photograph of him as a teenager standing beside a primitive electrical set-up he built in his father's house. He showed much aptitude for matters mechanical and electrical and at the age of 18 went to Vienna, having secured a position with a company called Bela Egger, makers of electrical equipment.

His background at Bela Egger stood him in good stead when, aged 23, he was offered a position by a Viennese coach-builder, Jacob Lohner. A carriage-maker who held a Royal Warrant, Lohner was drawn to the automobile but not those powered by petrol engines which were at the time rough, noisy and unreliable. He preferred the calm smoothness of the electric motor and

Right: A teenage
Ferdinand Porsche in
1894 with the
electrical system he
installed in his
father's house.

Far right: Porsche
aboard his
Semmering hill climb
record car. The
attempt at
streamlining (the
pointed nose) would
have been
outweighed by the
weight of the driver,
passenger and
batteries.

Below: By the late
1920s Porsche was
working for Daimler-
Benz and designing
such glorious
engines as this
straight six
supercharged device
fitted to the SSK.

made electrically powered cars under license from the French Jeantaud firm. In these early days there was no clear-cut distinction between the three major sources of power – electricity, gasoline or steam – and each offered particular advantages or disadvantages. Steam power had been fairly well developed but the machinery tended to be heavy and bulky, frequent stops were required en route to replenish water supplies and there was always the fear of explosions from the boiler. Electric motors were also well established but the batteries required to drive them – as true today as it was then – were bulky and heavy. A disproportionate amount of effort was dispelled in dragging them around. The gasoline engine, on the other hand, though not without faults, was in its infancy – which meant that it was being refined, improved and made more efficient almost daily. And, above all, the source of energy – gasoline – was highly concentrated. A compact, relatively light, tankful was all that was required.

Porsche was probably aware of all this but his electrical leanings came first. However, his ability to think laterally became apparent with his design for Lohner. Where others used a conventional drive from motor to wheels via clanking chains or flapping belts, Porsche deleted all this at a stroke by installing the motors in the wheels – in the front wheels, what's more, thus making him a pioneer of front-wheel drive. When the Lohner-Porsche was shown at the Paris exposition in 1900 it created much interest – and its designer was a mere 25 years old.

Realizing the disadvantages – the weight and bulk – of batteries, and the compact advantages of the gasoline engine, Porsche's next design took both into account. He replaced the batteries with a gasoline-engine-powered generator which in turn drove the motors in the wheels. This has to be considered an interim solution, since the weight of the generator and motors probably came to more than that of a conventional transmission system, but it did give a smooth take-up and did not require gear-changing dexterity on the part of the driver.

This *Mixte* system, as it was called, was a Porsche dead-end as far as the automobile was concerned, but it became popular where weight was not too much of a penalty. Buses and trucks were fitted with it, and indeed the London Fire Brigade was equipped with Lohner-Porsche fire engines. Probably the most spectacular application came with the land-train used by the Austrian army in World War I. This consisted of a tractor unit pulling a number of trailers, each of which was fitted with motor-in-hub wheels. Never mind four-wheel-drive, how about 40-or-more-wheel-drive? The advantages in heavy going were considerable. The Porsche *Mixte* system survives to this day on the railways. Significantly, although both pure electrical propulsion and the *Mixte* system would find their niche in heavy vehicles in years to come, they were competitive enough at the turn of

Above: One of the greatest and most charismatic sports cars ever, the SSK (and its sisters the SS and SSKL) dominated sports car racing in the late 1920s and early 1930s, including a prestigious win in the Mille Miglia in 1931. The Porsche 917 would repeat the SSK's success 40 years on.

the century for Porsche to go racing with them, achieving some successes in the process. Even with his first cars, the die was cast: competition in sporting events would always play a large part in Porsche lore. Publicity, of course, was important but the practical technical spin-offs could be even more so.

By 1905, Porsche had married Aloisia Johanna Kaes who had born him a daughter, Louise, in 1904. He was now working for a new master, Austro-Daimler, as technical director. Austro-Daimler, like the British Daimler company, was an offshoot of the Stuttgart company but was steadily going its own way. Porsche was a mere 30 years old at the time of his appointment, some indication of the value placed on his ability. He persevered for a while with the *Mixte* system but in 1909 he produced his first purely gasoline-engined car, a 32hp, four-cylinder machine. Naturally, he went racing with it, and it was while he was competing in the Semmering Hillclimb on Sunday 19 September 1909, that his son, Ferdinand Anton Ernst (first nicknamed Ferdy, later changed to Ferry) was born. Porsche Sr won his class that day and did not learn of his son's arrival until he got home. 'Most prophetic,' Ferry was to recall much later.

Porsche developed the model to such a pitch that it won the highly prestigious Prince Henry Trial in 1910. Subsequently, Prince Henry became an Austro-Daimler model name (Vauxhall in Britain did the same thing). His output at Austro-Daimler was prolific and multi-faceted: quite apart from cars, there were trucks and the land-

trains, not to mention an aero engine well before there was such a thing as an Austrian aircraft. This was an air-cooled flat-four: shades of things to come perhaps? In 1916 he was appointed managing director of the company. He had been showered with awards and one in particular was outstanding for someone with a fairly elementary establishment education: this was an honorary doctorate from the Technische Hochschule in Vienna.

The postwar years in Austria – like everywhere else – were tough. The move was to smaller cars, and Porsche was aware of this. However, in the summer of 1921 he went to a race meeting in Brescia in Italy, along with a friend, Count Kolowrat, and saw the delightful little Bugattis. His imagination was fired and on his return to Austria he soon produced a design for a small racing car. The engine was a 1100cc unit, featuring a single overhead camshaft and developing something like 40bhp. It was called the Sascha, after Count Kolowrat.

Four Saschas were entered for the tough Targa Florio in Sicily. Each car carried the sign for a suit of cards – clubs, diamonds, spades and hearts. The Sascha displaying the diamond won the 1100cc class, driven by someone who would become almost as famous as the doctor himself, Alfred Neubauer, later the legendary team manager for Daimler-Benz. This was all good publicity for the company, particularly when it was noted that the performance of the Sascha was out of all proportion to its size. Thus encouraged, a team was entered for a race at Monza the same year, 1922. This proved disastrous, the cars being unreliable with holed pistons, but, more tragically, one of the drivers, Fritz Kuhn, was killed in an accident. This was the sort of publicity the company could do without. Within any such establishment there will always be friction, and not for the last time the strong-willed doctor now found himself at loggerheads with the other directors.

Thus it was that in 1923 he left Austro-Daimler to take up the position of technical director (with a seat on the board) of the Daimler Motoren Gesellschaft in Stuttgart in southern Germany, replacing the ailing and overworked Paul Daimler. It was an exceedingly rough time in Germany's history with inflation totally out of control – it is reputed that the workers at the Daimler factory in Unterturkheim had to take their pay home in suitcases and that the company printed its own bank notes for millions of marks.

In spite of this, Daimler partook wholeheartedly in motor racing. The early 1920s also saw the emergence of the supercharger with its inherent ability to increase dramatically the power to weight ratio of engines. There was another advantage, though one perhaps less quantifiable – that of image. Like turbochargers a few years ago, superchargers were regarded as ultrahigh technology which, when cars so fitted won races, was valuable publicity.

Porsche's first job at Daimler was to take over a team of single-seaters destined for Indianapolis. These were four-cylinder 2-liter machines with such advanced features as a supercharger and four valves per cylinder but the doctor was not given enough time to perfect them and their showing was pretty dismal at the American event.

However, by 1924 they were reliable and powerful enough to come first in the Targa Florio, a victory which was to have other consequences.

When Porsche had arrived at Stuttgart, the snobbish Germans refused to recognize his honorary doctorate but after the Targa victory he was awarded a similar doctorate from the Stuttgart Technische Hochschule.

Another 2-liter machine followed, this time an eight-cylinder 32-valve blown device but its development was hampered not only by the economic climate but also by Count Zborowski's unfortunate death in one at Monza. However, a highly

Above: Porsche's *Mixte* (gasoline-electric) drive system was highly versatile. Power at each wheel gave it enormous advantages when used as an all-terrain vehicle, as in this Austrian army 'Landtrain.'

Left: A masked Alfred Neubauer, later to achieve fame as the team manager for Mercedes-Benz, poses in the little Sascha Austro-Daimler in which he won the 1100cc class in the 1922 Targa Florio.

talented youngster, Rudolf Caracciola, won the first postwar German Grand Prix (GP) at the Avus in 1926 driving the automobile. Of rather more significance was the fact that a few weeks after the Avus victory, Daimler and Benz amalgamated, the new company emerging with two chief engineers (the other being Benz man Hans Nibel), a situation which seldom if ever leads to a good working relationship.

Among his other duties, which included trucks and aero engines, Porsche was given the task of designing a new range of Mercedes cars, six-cylinder machines with capacities of 2, 4 and 6 liters. The flagship was the 6-liter model, designated in Germany the 24/100/140, in-house as the Type 600, and, to confuse matters, the 33/140 in England. The engine was a 6240cc straight-six with a light alloy block, a single overhead camshaft operating the valves through fingers and, of course, a supercharger. This was a Roots device, mounted up front of the engine, driven by a multi-disk clutch which engaged when the accelerator pedal was pushed right down to the floorboards: hence the 100/140 designation. Maximum power unblown was 100bhp, while maximum power with blower engaged was 140bhp. The chassis could best be described as pedestrian, belying the enormous, flexible exhaust pipes curling out of the hood which would become a trademark for the model and a styling cliché for a long time to come. Think of the Cord 810...

On this rather unlikely basis, Porsche and his colleagues set about making a proper sports car. Thus the model K appeared in 1927 with 14 inches chopped out of the chassis (K stood for *Kurz*, German for short). The performance was pretty sensational but the roadholding and handling were not, and this model became known as The Death Trap. It would accelerate from 10 to 30mph in a mere 3secs in second gear, but took 145 feet to stop from 40mph. However, the basis of a truly great car was there beneath the K's skin and in June 1927 the model S was introduced. This would turn out to be one of the finest sports cars ever built. For a start there was more power from a bigger engine – 6800cc and 180bhp. More importantly, the engine was moved back 14 inches and there was a new, low-line chassis with the rear semi-elliptic springs underslung beneath the axle and, thankfully, much more powerful brakes.

The first appearance of the S on a track coincided with the opening of one of the most famous racing circuits in the world, the Nürburgring, on 26 June 1927. Caracciola and Rosenberger drove two of the new models and promptly blew off everything in sight, erstwhile Grand Prix cars included. This would be just the first of innumerable wins recorded by Ss – 53 in 1928 alone.

However, 1928 saw the introduction of two of the most famous of all the derivatives, the SS and SSK. The biggest change under the hood came from yet another capacity increase to 7.1 liters, giving 140bhp (later 160bhp) in the unblown mode, and a nice, even, powerful 200bhp with blower engaged. Wheelbase for the SS was 11 feet 2 inches, and the bare chassis weighed some 33 cwt, so it was no lightweight. The SS received its baptism of fire at the 1928 German Grand Prix in July, Caracciola, Merz and Werner finishing 1-2-3. A bare ten days after this event the SSK appeared at the Gabelbach Hillclimb, Caracciola setting a new

record. It was appropriate that the SSK's first win should be in such an event since it was intended initially as a hillclimb special, and because of this the chassis was chopped yet again to a 9-foot 8-inch wheelbase. With the same engine capacity as the SS, but with a higher compression ratio, the SSK gave 170bhp unblown and 220bhp blown. There were also a couple of works racers, one of which gave 180bhp and 250bhp respectively, while the other, with the supercharger engaged full time, gave no less than 300 bhp.

The Ss, SSs, SSKs and the ultimate development of the theme, the lightweight SSKL, had a glorious competition career, dominating much of the sports-car racing in 1929, 1930 and 1931. Highlights included a win at the Newtonards Tourist Trophy (TT) in Ireland in 1929 and a first-time-out victory for the SSKL in the 1931 Mille Miglia driven by Caracciola, a feat recorded as one of the epic single-handed drives in the history of motor racing. These models were leviathans of the track – big, fast, massively brutal, almost throwbacks to the Edwardian era, but even in their heyday the writing was on the wall for this sort of car. Bugatti and Alfa Romeo had proved that smaller, more nimble, lighter, albeit less-powerful, machines were their equal and, on twistier circuits, faster.

Alas, Dr Porsche was not around at Daimler-Benz to savor the fruits of these victories. After the merger, the combined Daimler and Benz board opted for more conservative designs from Benz for their mass-produced cars, stolid side-valve devices that were worthy but unexciting. On the last day of 1928 another notable event occurred: Porsche left Daimler-Benz after the almost inevitable blazing row. Nevertheless, as the historian Bunty Scott-Moncrieff observed: 'Porsche should be given the greatest credit for the development of supercharged engines, which he initiated and carried through during his time with Mercedes.'

Below: A young Ferry Porsche poses behind the wheel of the second VW ever built, and the first convertible, with his wife Dorothea beside him and a friend, Hellmuth Zarges, behind.

Above left: Three generations of the Porsche family with the Doctor in the middle flanked by Ferry (left) and grandson Peter (right).

Left: The fabled 1936 Auto-Union was a joint Ferdinand/Ferry design.

While at Daimler-Benz, Porsche had commissioned a large villa in the Feuerbacherweg, in Stuttgart, a house that was to become home to the Porsche family from then on. But on his departure from Daimler-Benz, he moved back to Austria, to Steyr, as chief engineer, letting the villa on the Feuerbacherweg to his erstwhile co-director Hans Nibel. At Steyr he was responsible for two models, a large straight-eight luxury device, the Austria, and a smaller 2-liter, the Type 30, which featured swing axles at the rear but which was otherwise fairly conventional. His stay at Steyr was brief but not because of his inability to get on with the management: this time Steyr's bankers went broke and were taken over by the group that financed Austro-Daimler. In the reshuffle the Austria was dropped while Austro-Daimler, not perhaps too surprisingly, cancelled Porsche's three-year contract with two years still to run.

With his years of experience and brilliant reputation as an engineer, Dr Porsche could have taken up a number of positions with other companies (at Skoda in Pilsen for example) but at the age of 54 he was tired of company intrigues. The idea of setting up his own consultancy business was not a blinding inspiration, for he had been considering it for some time, but here at last was the opportunity to put his dreams into practice.

Since Stuttgart was near enough the center of the motor industry for the German-speaking world and the area in which he had most contacts, it was logical to open his new establishment there. Accordingly he moved back and in April 1931 the Porsche Konstruktionbüro für Motoren-Fahrzeug, Luftfahrzeug und Wasserfahrzeugbau came into being. With a name like that, the doctor's motto could have been 'You name it, we'll design it'!

He gathered around him a select band of individuals, all Austrian. There was Karl Rabe, an engineer who had been with Porsche at Austro-Daimler; Erwin Kommenda, the body man; Joseph Mickl, the aerodynamacist and walking calculator; and Porsche's son Ferry, then a 21-year-old stripling. His son-in-law, a Viennese lawyer called Anton Piëch, came in as a partner. Another partner was Adolf Rosenberger.

Life for the first couple of years of the Porsche design bureau was very much on a hand-to-mouth basis, though the first commission for the new office in the Kronenstrasse came in fairly rapidly. It was for a 2-liter Wanderer and was arbitrarily given the project number Type 7, so as not to appear to be the very first. This was a straightforward machine and went into production just before Wanderer merged with Audi, Horch and DKW to form Auto Union.

Of more historical significance in the light of what was to follow was the project number Type 12. This arose through a contract from the Zündapp motorcycle firm which was going through a

rough patch. Zündapp's head, Fritz Neumeyer, tried to expand into the cheap car market and went to Porsche for a suitable design. Three prototypes were designed and built before motorcycle sales grew and Neumeyer cancelled the project. But the significance lies in the design of the Type 12. It was rear-engined for a start, though the power unit was a 1200cc five-cylinder radial. Then there was independent suspension all round and a streamlined body designed by Kommenda and built by Reutter. At first – and second – glance it could be a study for the Volkswagen (VW).

To show Porsche's stature in the automotive world, he was approached by a mysterious gentleman in 1932 with an offer to go to Russia to study its motor industry. He accepted and while on tour was offered the position of head of the whole outfit. Tempting though the suggestion was, it was never considered too seriously by the doctor.

With the Type 12, Porsche had shown his ability to think laterally again for it was as far removed from the SSs and SSKs as you could get. It was followed by the Type 32, a design for yet another motorcycle manufacturer, NSU. This was, if anything, an even closer prototype of the VW, for it featured an air-cooled flat-four engine in the tail, Porsche's own independent suspension at the front via torsion bars and trailing arms (patented in 1932), and independent suspension again at the rear also via swing axles and torsion bars. The chassis consisted of a tubular central backbone with metal panels outrigged on either side to take

the bodywork. Clothing it was another sleek Kommenda shape. Once more, three prototypes were built before the project was cancelled. One of these survives in the VW Museum at Wolfsburg.

One project, the Type 22, did not start from an outside approach. This was for a single-seater racer to meet the new Grand Prix regulations which had been agreed upon internationally in 1932. These set a minimum weight limit of 750 kg but with no limit on engine capacity. The Porsche solution was radical. The engine was a V16 with three camshafts to operate the 32 valves: the central camshaft worked the exhaust valves via pushrods, the two outer ones the inlets directly. With an initial output of 250bhp from 4.5 liters, it was capable of some considerable expansion, eventually giving 600bhp from 6 liters, thanks in part to some pretty impressive supercharging. The most radical part of the car, however, was the layout, for the engine was mounted behind the driver and fuel tank but in front of the rear wheels.

Every Grand Prix car today follows this practice but in the 1930s it was regarded as very *avant-garde* indeed. The reasons for such a layout as propounded by Ferry Porsche nowadays seem fairly obvious: a lower frontal area since the transmission system did not have to fight its way past or under the driver; better balance since, with the fuel tank in the middle, the automobile's handling should be the same whether the tank was full or empty; and, with the deletion of some of the transmission, it would give an optimum power-to-

the drawing board and good contacts with the newly-formed Auto Union group. An approach was made to the group who rather liked the idea and agreed to take up the Type 22 provided they received part of the sponsorship. A delegation, which included the doctor, was formed to approach Herr Hitler. Porsche was, of course, quite famous but was somewhat astounded when Hitler reminded him that they had met before at a race meeting at the Solitude in 1925. This, and the fact that the Porsche design was already on the drawing board, swayed the Chancellor, and the sponsorship was split between the two rival companies.

weight ratio. In practice, however, the engine was quite a sizable lump in its own right with negative results on frontal area, while Mercedes achieved a very similar power-to-weight ratio with a more conventional design. As for the handling characteristics, they may have been constant but they were also constantly tricky and very few could drive them near their limit. One who could, Bernd Rosemeyer, an ex-motorcyclist, did so brilliantly, but he was tragically killed while attempting some record breaking on the Frankfurt autobahn in 1938 when his car was blown off course. Another was the legendary Tazio Nuvolari, the tiny Mantuan, who could drive anything quickly. A third was Hans Stuck Snr, father of the present Porsche racing driver.

On 30 January 1933, one of the most fateful events in world history took place: Adolf Hitler became Chancellor of Germany. One of his first acts was to put up a 600,000 DM fund to sponsor a German Grand Prix car. Daimler-Benz, with their wealth of experience on the track, were expected to walk away with it, but the Porsches had their Type 22 on

From then until the outbreak of World War II, Mercedes-Benz and Auto Union would dominate Grand Prix racing, the highest form of motor sport in what has come to be regarded as the golden age of motor racing. Anyone who has seen either a Mercedes or Auto Union in action, even on a demonstration run, will understand why it was so called. (There is a curious postscript to the Auto Union story. In the late 1930s Porsche was approached by Daimler-Benz, Auto Union's deadly rivals, to design a land-speed record breaker for them. Developed, somewhat naturally, in the greatest secrecy, it was built but World War II intervened before it could run. Here was a perfect example of what the Porsche design studio would become famous for, a case of the left hand knowing perfectly well what the right hand was doing but not letting on to anyone else . . .)

Hitler's dreams in the motoring field ran to greater things than simple domination of the racing circuits of the world. An admirer of Henry Ford, he wanted to put the German people on wheels as Ford had done for the Americans. It is on record that, as early as 1924, he was talking about a small mass-produced car for the common man to go with his great scheme to build thousands of miles of autobahn which would not only improve communications but also mop up the vast numbers of unemployed.

3 Weltrekorde für Deutschland

DER **AUTO UNION** RENNWAGEN

stellte am 6. III. 34 auf der Avus bei Berlin folgende neue Weltbestzeiten auf

für 100 MEILEN . . . . . . 216,869 KILOMETER

für 200 KILOMETER . . . 217,085 KILOMETER

in 1 STUNDE . . . . . . 217,106,79 km

AUDI · DKW · HORCH · WANDERER

Hitler's motoring adviser was an old friend and a director of Daimler-Benz, Jacob Werlin, from whom Hitler had bought his first car. In late 1933 Werlin called on Porsche at the Kronenstrasse offices, and this was followed up a few days later by a meeting between Hitler, Porsche and Werlin. It was at this meeting that Hitler laid down the essential characteristics he required from a 'People's car.' It should be capable of carrying four adults, have a top speed of 100kph (62mph), give some 42mpg, be air-cooled, and simple to service and repair. And one other thing: it should cost no more than DM 1000, worth then about £90 or $350.

With this brief, the Porsche bureau set to work. Not surprisingly, project Type 60, as it was numbered in-house, bore strong similarities to the aborted NSU Type 32. Detailed work began in early 1934 and in May of that year Hitler was shown the preliminary drawings. There is on record a sketch showing the changes he made to the nose. He may also have been one of the first to call it a Beetle, for it is also on record that he said, 'It should look like a beetle – you've only got to look to nature to find out what streamlining is.'

It is beyond dispute that Dr Porsche and his team fathered the VW. That they fathered the concept is much more open to debate. We tend to think of the VW as totally different from anything else made at the time but this was not so. There was in the 1920s and 1930s a group of talented designers from what we will call Middle Europe. They included Porsche himself, Hans Ledwinka who explored similar ideas at Tatra, Rumpler of Tropfenwagen fame, and Joseph Ganz, the editor of the influential *Motor-Kritik* magazine. They all at one time or another pursued the theme of 'streamlined' cars with engines in the tail, swing-axle suspension, and backbone-type chassis. In fact, Ledwinka had led the way in the early 1920s with the Tatra Type 11 which, though it had a front-mounted engine and conventional bodywork, featured a central tube chassis and swing axles at the

rear. In 1933 the Standard Superior, a Ganz design, was in production, following in spirit if not detail the Middle European ideas. Rumpler had, in the mid-1920s, shown his Tropfenauto, though his aerodynamics were more of the vertical than the horizontal variety (it was only when viewed from above that the teardrop shape after which it was named was obvious) and this was followed by the famous Tropfenwagen racer. This must, incidentally, have had some influence on the Auto Union since it was one of the first mid-engined, streamlined racing cars ever made, though perhaps the influence was more negative than positive. In the same year Ledwinka designed a small car that was a dead ringer for the VW, but it never progressed beyond the prototype stage. Finally, in 1933 and 1934 Daimler-Benz introduced their Types 130, 150 and 170, three more VW dead ringers except that they used water-cooled in-line four cylinder engines.

Thus there was a fair amount of similar work going on at the same time, and Porsche was nothing if not eclectic. A case of plagiarism, or was it great minds thinking alike? The most likely explanation is that they were all from the same neck of the woods, that they knew each other and knew of each others' work. The characteristics of the cars were influenced by the conditions then prevailing in the area. Independent suspension meant that they could cope with the rough secondary roads. The engine in the back gave better grip in slippery conditions and kept the noise away from the passenger compartment. Streamlining would give higher speeds and better consumption on the new types of high-speed freeways then coming into existence. None of this, though, detracts from Porsche's work. It was his drive and energy, and Hitler's backing, that pushed the concept into the mass-production field. The others fell by the wayside: Porsche's ideas endured.

From 1934 until World War II, Dr Porsche became more and more involved with the VW project which tended to be delayed for one reason or another. He eventually became a director and one of the two managers of Volkswagenwerke GmbH. The early days of the Beetle, and its subsequent lengthy history, have been well chronicled elsewhere: let us just remember that it was indeed a Porsche inspiration.

However, the Porsches being the Porsches (by the late 1930s Ferry was playing a far greater part in the running of the company), although the VW project was taking up a great deal of their attention, they still had time for other projects, some of which had a direct bearing on the Porsche story. One that didn't was the Type 52, a three-abreast sports car based on the Auto Union Grand Prix car. Now that would have been a machine . . . Then there was the Type 114, a most intriguing device with a mid-engine layout. The most unusual feature of this sports car (which, like the Type 52, never saw production) was the engine, a

Below: Shortly before his death, Ferdinand Porsche is toasted by his son Ferry (left) and the Mercedes-Benz racing driver Rudolf Caracciola.

V10 no less, of 1500cc capacity. Then there was the Type 64, an aluminum-bodied sports car based on VW mechanicals, with the engine enlarged to 1.5 liters.

Probably the most significant was the 60K10. This was another Beetle variant but designed for a specific purpose: to compete in a race organized by the German head of sport, *Korpsführer* Hühnlein. This was to celebrate the Nazi Axis, so not unnaturally it was to run from Berlin to Rome, taking in much of the newly completed *Autobahnen* and *Autostrada*, a high-speed dash from one capital city to another. The VW platform and suspension was retained intact but the engine was worked over to give more power, about 50bhp, while Kommenda designed a stunningly beautiful new body for it. This was amazingly svelte, even the front wheels being enclosed in spats, while the cockpit was so tight that the passenger's seat had to be staggered backwards so that two people could fit in it. Three cars were built to this specification for the race which was due to take place in September 1939 but other more pressing matters intervened and it was cancelled. However, one was put to good use: the Porsches used it as high-speed transport throughout the war. It was later bought by the one-armed racing driver Otto Mathé, and survives to this day.

When World War II broke out, the Porsche bureau turned to designing military vehicles. The Type 82 *Kubelwagen* is a well-known example,

and became to the Germans what the Jeep was to the Allies. Then there was the *Schwimmwagen*, the amphibious version of the *Kubelwagen*, and assorted tanks, some of which used the *Mixte* drive system that Porsche had pioneered. The most notorious was the mighty *Maus*, a vast 180-ton land battleship which never saw production, while the most famous was the Type 101, the Tiger. Not all the contracts were for military machinery: Types 135, 136 and 137 were for wind-powered generators, while Types 110-113 were for a simple – the word 'primitive' could almost be applied – tractor to replace horses for ploughing. In 1940 Dr Porsche was made an honorary professor by the Stuttgart Technische Hochschule, and briefly he was head of the Armor Commission under Albert Speer. However, dare one say that his lack of tact and his desire for fine engineering rather than knife-and-fork mass-production methods, necessary to keep the forces topped up with equipment, saw him shifted upwards and sideways to become a consultant on armaments.

A new office cum factory and test center had been opened at Zuffenhausen, a suburb of Stuttgart, in 1938 to cope with the increased work load of the Porsche company, and in 1944 a bomb fell on it, doing relatively little damage except to destroy some records. The significance of this was that it became obvious that Stuttgart was becoming a dangerous place to be, so alternative sites were sought. Being at heart Austrian, the family

Above: The Type 32, a design study for the motorcycle manufacturer NSU, predates the VW but still features an air-cooled flat four engine in the tail, independent suspension all round and a 'streamlined' body. A VW prototype perhaps?

looked to the area near their country home at Zell-am-See near Salzburg. A gliding school was found and taken over, but it was too small so another site was also taken over, a former sawmill in a tiny village called Gmünd. Miles from anywhere, it was at least safe from bombs.

By all accounts it seems that the Porsche family's political affiliations lay nowhere in particular. Neither the Professor nor Ferry were ever members of the Nazi Party, and, though honors were heaped on them, not all were welcome: Ferry, for example, was made a colonel in the SS, a meaningless move by Himmler since the last thing Ferry wanted was to wear a uniform and strut around – he is on record as having an abiding hatred of all uniforms. Furthermore, when it was pointed out to Hitler that the Professor was Czechoslovakian, the Führer 'granted' him German nationality. There was nothing the doctor could do about it but he considered himself Austrian right to the end.

When the war ended, the three sections of the Porsche organization were split between the Americans and the British, one suspects rather to their relief – the alternative might have been a forced acceptance by the Professor of the offer the Russians had made years before. The family themselves were at Zell-am-See under the Americans, Gmünd came under the Germans, and Zuffenhausen was the other in the American sector. In the initial hiatus, Karl Rabe, the retiring chief designer, was put in charge of Gmünd by the British, while Karl Kirn headed the Zuffenhausen offices which were taken over by the American armed forces as a motor pool, and which would not be returned for many years.

In August 1945 the Professor was interned in a castle near Frankfurt under Operation Dustbin, the name given to an operation investigating prominent Germans. He was not there for very long, eventually being cleared of any possible potential charges since he was so obviously apolitical (Albert Speer spoke in his defense, putting the point to the Allies) and he was allowed to return home. Ferry, Anton Piëch and other members of the Porsche organization had also been arrested a little earlier but they too had been released.

However, matters did not end there. In November 1945 the Professor was approached by the French. His brief: design a Volkswagen for them. There were a couple of meetings at which the Professor, Ferry and Piëch met with the Germans at Baden-Baden where nothing much was settled and then, in mid-December, all three were arrested on the orders of the French Minister of Justice. Ferry was released after only a few months but the Professor and Piëch were jailed for over twenty months in Paris and Dijon. Apart from the consequences of imprisonment itself, conditions were not exactly first class and the effects on the Professor's health were near disastrous.

Quite what it was all about was never fully ex-

plained, but the French come out of the whole affair rather badly. Part of the reason seems to have been that the entrenched French motor industry did not want a French Volkswagen – there was enough competition between Renault, Citroën and Peugeot as it was – and it was they who arranged the incarceration. Another reason was that there was much political in-fighting in France at the time, and those parties opposed to Marcel Paul, then Minister of Industrial Production who had made the approach to Porsche, applied pressure to his rival, Pierre Teitgen, the Minister of Justice who signed the arrest warrant. There may even have been a third, and rather more sinister reason. Pierre Peugeot was the one who brought charges against Porsche, and this was most curious since the Germans had taken over the Peugeot factories during the war to make VW components. The Professor had been a regular visitor to the factory, he and the Frenchman apparently being on amicable terms with each other. In fact, Porsche had intervened with the infamous Gestapo at one point after some Peugeot

Above: Versatility was the name of the Porsche game, as evinced by this 1940 *Volkstraktor,* intended as a cheap replacement for the horse.

personnel were arrested on sabotage charges. Some saw Peugeot's war-crime charges as an attempt to divert attention away from himself, to forestall any possible collaboration charges he might have had to face. Whatever the reasons, it was not until August 1947 that the Professor was released, tired and dispirited.

While the male members of the family were in prison, the running of the only working Porsche establishment, the saw-mill at Gmünd, was taken over by the strong-willed daughter of the Professor, Louise Piëch, helped by Rabe, but on his return in July 1946 Ferry took over the reins. They still had a considerable number of employees on their staff but work in the shattered remains of the Third Reich was an almost unobtainable commodity. Work they found, however, such as making and repairing farm equipment, and ex-army VWs. They were kept reasonably busy but nevertheless 1946 must have been a very bad year for Porsche.

Matters took an upturn in late 1946, with the request to design a new racing car for an Italian industrialist, Piero Dusio. This contract came in a roundabout way. Anton Piëch's secretary had married a Viennese racing motorcyclist, Karl (later called Carlo) Abarth, who had emigrated to Italy where he met an ex-Porsche employee, Rudolf Hruska, stranded in Italy after the war. Both, of course, would go on to become famous names, Abarth as a tuner and manufacturer of racing cars, and Hruska as the father of the Alfasud.

They had corresponded with the Porsches after the war, and Ferry had offered them representation of Porsche interests in Italy. The catalyst between Abarth, Hruska, Porsche and Dusio was none other than Tazio Nuvolari, who was familiar with Porsche potential from his Auto Union days. Dusio, who had made his fortune during the war making boots for the army, had sprung into action in 1946, constructing cheap sports cars and single-seaters under the Cisitalia name, thus in effect bringing the sport back into life and giving the Italians a lead which they were to hold in the field

Above: A rather morose Ferdinand Porsche (with hat in front) sits on yet another example of his creative abilities, a 1943 Elephant tank.

Below: Arguably the first true Porsche prototype, the 60K10 VW variant, designed for the Berlin-Rome race, featured a tuned VW engine and stunningly sleek, aerodynamically clean, aluminum bodywork to allow it to cruise at very high speed.

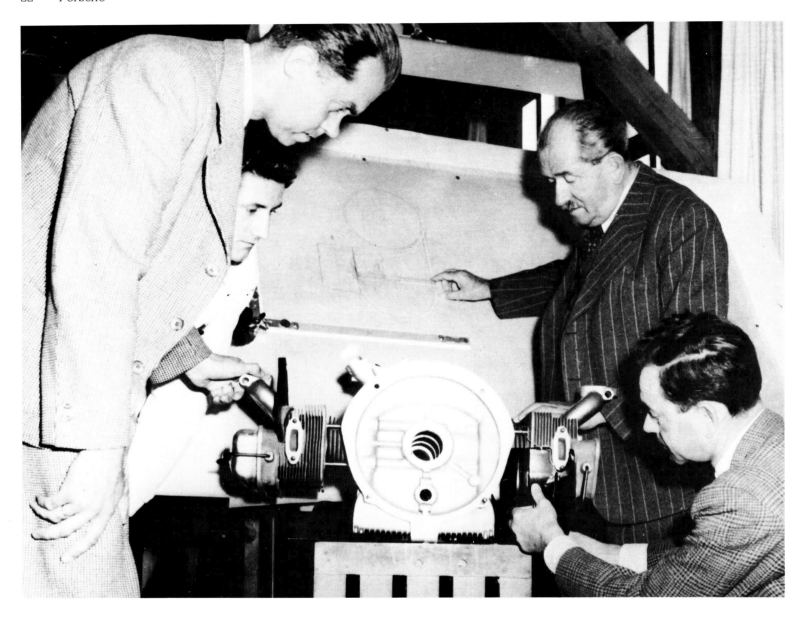

Above: One of the last pictures taken of the Professor at Zuffenhausen shortly before his death, discussing a wooden mock-up of a Type 356 engine with Ferry (kneeling, right) and other Porsche technicians.

Right: A Porsche Type 166, otherwise known as a VW-*Schwimmwagen*, the amphibious version of the German Jeep, the Type 82 *Kubelwagen*.

Above: In the beginning – this is the very first car to bear the Porsche name. It was a low, aluminum-bodied roadster with the engine in the middle, and appeared in 1948.

for some years to come. When the idea of a Porsche-designed Grand Prix car was put to him, he jumped at the chance.

Ferry, Rabe and the others set to on the Cisitalia project. Even by today's standards it was ambitious. It was, of course, mid-engined, powered by a supercharged flat 12 of 1.5-liters capacity with a potential output of 450bhp. In addition, provision was made for part-time four-wheel-drive. Naturally, torsion-bar suspension was used all round. One complete car, and parts for another, were completed by 1949, but by then Dusio's company was in financial difficulties. Dusio was invited by the President of Argentina, Peron, to instigate an Argentinian motor industry, and the Grand Prix project was transferred to South America, where it reappeared under a new name, Autocar. The one complete car practiced for a race but did not start, and then deranged itself while attempting some speed records. That was the end of that, except that the complete car was discovered in 1959, bought by Porsche and restored, and it is now residing in their museum. The remaining parts of the other car were bought by Tom Wheatcroft and built up for display in his Donington Collection.

Though the Type 360, as the Cisitalia was called, was one of the less-successful Porsche designs, the fees raised were enough to pay the bail demanded by the French for the release of the Professor, so some good came out of it.

While the Professor was in jail and the Cisitalia project on the boil, Ferry instigated another in-house project, given the Type number 356. It is all the more ironic that the only car to bear the name of Porsche was born in the Professor's absence. In the last couple of years of his life, in ill health for much of that time, Professor Ferdinand Porsche threw himself into the fledgling car-manufacturing company, but the real credit for getting it off the ground must go to Ferry. In November 1950 Ferdinand Anton Porsche suffered a stroke from which he never fully recovered and he died in January 1951. With his death ended the first part of the Porsche story, but by then the second part, as manufacturers of fine cars, was well on its way.

He was not to know the glories which the name of Porsche would reap in the years ahead, but he must have known that the principles and virtues he had instilled in all those who were associated with him would live on.

PORSCHE HITS THE ROAD: THE 356

The number 356 is hardly memorable. It doesn't roll off the tongue, it doesn't sound poetic, it doesn't conjure up visions of sinewed wild cats, it might be the most anonymous number you can think of between 1 and 1000. Yet to motoring enthusiasts in general, and Porscheophiles in particular, those three digits have a very special significance. They were applied to one of the greatest sports cars the world has ever seen: the Porsche 356. The origins of the number are, of course, quite prosaic. It simply means Porsche project Type 356, a design for a tourer based on VW mechanicals.

While on a visit to Piero Dusio's establishment to oversee the Grand Prix car project, Ferry Porsche and Karl Rabe had taken in the Italian's version of a cheap, small sports car, based on readily available Fiat components. A momentous and long-reaching decision was taken: Porsche would make a sports car. Not design one for someone else but make it themselves. They had the ability to carry out all the necessary work, including very low-volume production at Gmünd. And, just as Dusio based his car on those components which were most readily available, Porsche would base his on the VW. After all, he had initiated and been responsible for its birth: what better? In fact, he

Above: It could only be a 356. This is a typical example of the model, being in fact a 1958 A, and is unusual only in being fitted with a sun roof.

Previous pages: A line-up of early models (mostly 356s, but a rare 550 Spyder lurks at the left of the second row) during a meeting of the Porsche Owners Club in Great Britain.

Right: One of the very first, Gmünd-built, alloy-bodied coupés. Distinguishing features include the flat-plane windshield and small curved front quarter-lights.

Below: Beautiful it wasn't, purposeful it most certainly was. The 356 Speedster, due to its light weight, became the darling of the race tracks and one of the all-time collectable 356s. Flared rear arches on this example are non-standard.

Above: An early (1952) 356 Cabrio gave open-air motoring to those Porsche fans who required it.

Below: The traditional 356 engine bay, with most of the power unit hidden beneath the cooling fan and ducting.

might have had to look elsewhere: in the immediate aftermath of the war it was not obvious that there would be such a thing as a VW, but Wolfsburg had fallen into British hands and, with a handful of officers in charge, VWs had slowly and hesitatingly started to roll off the assembly lines. Over 10,000 had been built in 1946 and nearly 9000 in 1947: the Beetle entered history and with it the possibility of a VW-based Porsche sports car.

Project 356 was initiated on 11 June 1947 and by mid-July many of the drawings had been completed. These called for a tubular space frame *à la* Cisitalia, a VW engine reversed in the chassis so that it sat between seats and rear axle (it was, therefore, mid-engined), and VW suspension front and rear. Since the engine was now sitting where the transverse torsion bars would normally be placed, the whole rear suspension was reversed along with the engine/transmission package, which meant that the torsion bars were right in the tail of the car, held in a special frame structure, and that the trailing arms became leading arms. Front suspension was pure VW, with twin transverse tubes carrying the torsion bars, and twin trailing arms each side.

Above: A real wolf in sheep's clothing — only the badging on the tail tells you that this 1964 356 is, in fact, a Carrera 2 and thus capable of eating ostensibly more powerful machinery for breakfast. . . .

Right: The earliest 356s were the cleanest — this lovely 1951 example shows off the excellent aerodynamics, including the low-mounted, flush bumper which is very much in vogue nowadays.

Right: By the early 1960s, when this Cabrio was current, bumpers had taken on greater proportions to cope with growing traffic densities and parking by ear.

Below: The 356C was the last of the line, and hid disk brakes behind those plain hub caps.

Powering the car, of course, was a VW 1131cc flat-four air-cooled engine. Since its 25bhp was hardly going to endow anything with a startling performance – and certainly not a sports car – the head was mildly modified via larger inlet valves and ports and the compression ratio was increased from 5.8:1 to 7.0:1, fairly high considering the quality of fuel then available in that part of the world. When it was later fitted with twin carburetors, it gave some 40bhp, a nice, healthy increase.

Following initial tests by Ferry himself and Professor Eberan von Eberhorst (who had been responsible for the later Auto Union racers before World War II, and who would go on to design sports-racing cars for Aston Martin in England), the bare chassis received its body. Designed by Kommenda, it was as simple and as streamlined as you could get. Made of hand-beaten aluminum, it started with a simple bumper at the bottom of the nose, flared up and over, taking in the VW headlamps on the way, and then swept back with an almost straight fender line to the smooth tail. Both sets of wheels were deeply inset, the windshield was a simple two-pane affair, and, apart from a couple of chrome strips across the nose and the name PORSCHE front and rear (in a script that is still used to this day), there was no extraneous adornment at all. The interior was fairly spartan, with a bench seat whose shaped backrest gave a little lateral support, and minimal door trim and instrumentation.

Porsche number 1 was completed in May 1947 and was taken on an extended test session by Ferry, during which the tube supporting the torsion bar housing was bent. Two U-shaped metal bars were found and attached to strengthen the

Left: Sans bumpers and hub caps, but complete with miniscule windshield, the Speedster (this is a 1955 example) looks rarin' to go.

Below: Luggage space up front was strictly limited in a 356, the spare and fuel tank taking up most of the room. Owners used the space behind the seats instead.

Above: Raising the roof on a Speedster did nothing whatever for its looks – or the view out!

Left: The author enjoying himself immensely in a beautifully preserved 1956 'Damen' Cabrio. For its day, its road manners (except on the limit) were astonishingly good.

Right: The dashboard of a British spec 356 – it's right hand drive, for a start, and the speedometer is marked in mph, while the tachometer, red-lined at 6000rpm, indicates that it could be a Carrera (or at least a late model).

tube and these became part of the car's permanent structure. That was the only failure during the test session.

Shortly after that the car was taken for its first public airing to Switzerland, where it was driven by a number of journalists. In one of the first-recorded comments about it, Max Troesch wrote in *The Motor* that it had 'really remarkable road holding combined with a pleasant softness of springing and very light, accurate steering'. Already the compliments were flowing.

The effect of the car visually can be imagined. Almost every sports car on the road at the time came from pre-war days, which meant separate fenders and headlamps and vertical radiators – the

Right: The Zuffenhausen assembly line, with 356As rolling along.

Right: Porsche and competition were soon synonymous. This is Rudolf Sauerwein on his way to an overall second in the 1953 Alpine rally.

Below right: March 1956, and a garlanded 356 marks the 10,000th Porsche. A proud Ferry stands on the left.

Below: The grandmother of all competition Porsches, a Gmünd coupé with a lowered roof line: behind it stands Porsche's development engineer Wilhelm Hild. This particular car survives in Porsche's museum to this day.

T-series MGs will give you an idea of what they were like. One of the first truly modern sports cars, the Jaguar XK120, did not appear on the scene until October 1948, and the nearest to anything like the Porsche, with its simple, full-width bodywork, was the work of some of the Italian coach-builders on Maserati and Ferrari chassis. The Italians, in fact, have a word for the shape: *barchetta*, meaning little boat. The name was given to any light, open, sporting two-seater, the most famous being the Ferrari 166, but it could never have been used more appropriately than for that very first Porsche. It looked exactly like an upturned dinghy and if you think that sounds odd today, consider how much more odd it must have sounded and looked back in the late 1940s. (This, the prototype of all Porsches, was sold to a Swiss who owned an advertising agency, von Senger. He took it over in late 1948 but sold it back to Porsche in 1953. It now holds pride of place in the Porsche Museum.)

Concurrent with the prototype, however, Type 356/2 was taking shape. This was to be the definitive Porsche car and differed radically from number 1. Ferry had realized that space frames, though ideal for one-offs and Italian artisans, were less than ideal for mass production. In addition, the reversed rear suspension led to unacceptable loads in the wrong place – right in the tail of the car – and unwanted toe-out of the rear wheel when cornering due to the action of the leading, rather than trailing, arms. The mid-engined layout also took up a large amount of space that could be usefully used for luggage.

Thus the 356/2 reverted to a traditional VW layout, with the engine overslung out behind the rear axle. In place of the tubular space frame there was a structural sheet-steel platform with sills down the side and a small central tunnel to take the gear linkage and wiring, a boxed scuttle and footwell up front, and another structure at the back to hold the engine and rear suspension. Kommenda was again responsible for the shape and designs were drawn up for both open and closed bodywork, the latter getting preferential treatment since it was envisaged that the major sales outlets for Porsches would be central and northern Europe with their cold climate. The bodies were, like that of the prototype, hand-beaten from aluminum, and this was to cause something of a holdup in production to the extent that some of the early 356s were sent to Switzerland in chassis form. Why Switzerland? Because von Senger, and his partner, a car dealer called Bernhard Blank from Zurich, had ordered no less than 50 cars after a sight of the 356/2 in mock-up form. With their ability to travel more-or-less freely, and the fact that various parts could be ordered and paid for through Switzerland, something not possible to the Austrians, they could in effect be said to have put Porsche on their feet and got the whole ball rolling.

Production at Gmünd was erratic and a mere 50 or so cars were built there between 1948 and March 1951. Some were fitted with engines bearing the standard VW capacity of 1131cc but the majority featured a smaller bore, 73.5mm as against 75mm, to bring the capacity down to 1086cc and thus allow the cars to enter the 1100cc class in motor racing. Later models featured a

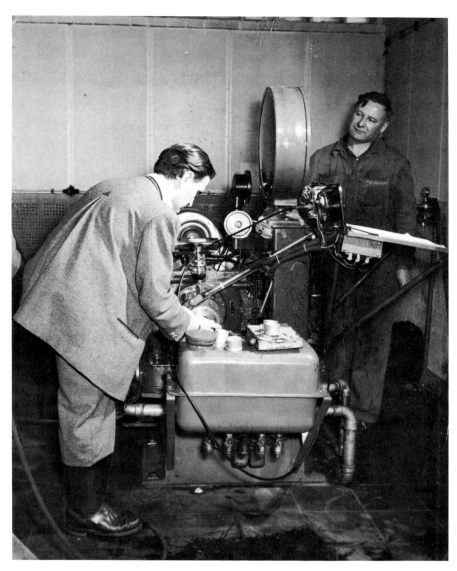

Above: A behind-the-scenes glimpse at Zuffenhausen in 1954, with Ernst Fuhrmann, later head of Porsche, supervising an engine test session.

Left: Occasional attempts were made to redesign the 356 outside of the works – this is the Swiss company Beutler's offering from 1959. Those tail fins date it badly, unlike the standard offering which was timeless.

special cylinder head in which the exhaust valves were angled outward toward the front and rear of the engine, thus giving better breathing via larger valves and smoother porting (the standard VW head suffered from chronic asthma in the interests of long life). In this form, with a compression ratio of 6.5:1, the 1100s could give some 40bhp at 4200rpm. Of the cars built at Gmünd, roughly half were coupés and half cabriolets, most of the latter being bodies by Beutler of Switzerland. One big customer was Scania-Vabis in Sweden – a truck manufacturer and the Swedish agent for VW, so a Porsche franchise was a logical addition to their stable. Another Porsche milestone was reached in March 1949: two Porsches, one a yellow Gmünd coupé, the other a Beutler cabrio, went on display at the Geneva Motor Show, marking their and the company's international show debut.

It became obvious that Gmünd, miles from anywhere and really nothing more than a collection of huts, was not the ideal place to make cars. There were, of course, the premises in Zuffenhausen but these were occupied by the Americans. They were paying rent which gave the company some useful income. Another source was VW: Ferry had been in touch with the head of VW, Heinz Nordhoff, about the supply of components to Pors-

che, and this led to some meetings which culminated in an agreement signed in September 1948. Under this, VW were to pay Porsche a royalty on every VW made and would keep them on a retainer as consultants; in return Porsche agreed not to design a competitive car for any other company. Another part of the agreement gave Porsche the franchise for VWs in Austria: this was to lead to Porsche-Salzburg under Anton Piëch and, after his death, Louise.

With all this income piling up in Germany and nothing to offset against tax, plus the impossibility of manufacturing cars at Gmünd, it became clear that there was only one reasonable solution: to move the car operation to Germany. The logical move was to the premises at Spitalwaldstrasse in Zuffenhausen, but the Americans were still ensconced there. Nevertheless, a small design team was installed in the garage and in a couple of rooms at the family home in the Feuerbacherweg. No production work could possibly be carried out there. However, just down the road from the Spitalwaldstrasse establishment there was the old-established coach-building firm of Reutter who had built some of the bodies for the pre-war prototype Beetles and the three aluminum shells for the Berlin-Rome cars. They were well-known to

Right: The Brighton Speed Trials in England (a sort of drag race for sporting machinery) showed just how advanced the Porsche was in its day compared to its contemporaries such as the MG TD on the right.

Below: By 1958 the 356 was not only fast but also refined and civilized – this Cabrio incorporates all modern conveniences.

Porsche and had an excellent reputation. Getting Reutter to build the bodies would remove the biggest bottleneck in 356 production. Reutter also had some available space within their grounds which Porsche could rent and in which assembly of complete cars could take place. In November 1949 Porsche placed an order with Reutter for 500 bodies, to be made of steel in the interests of costs and ease of manufacture.

The first Reutter-built shell was completed early in 1950 for the Porsche family, father and son, to see. The Professor created something of a sensation when, after looking at it long and hard for a while, declared it to be asymmetrical. He was right: one side was out by less than an inch, but out nevertheless.

On the day before Easter 1950 the first German-built Porsche made its official appearance. This and subsequent cars differed subtly from the Gmünd cars, the most visual change being to the side windows: on the Gmünd coupés there were small, curved quarter lights, which were replaced by flat glass in the Stuttgart cars. To keep the flow of air around the glass house smooth, the outer ends of the two-piece windshield were curved instead.

In October 1950 Porsches were displayed at Paris for the first time, in front of a banner which reminded everyone just how long Porsche had been around: it simply said 1900 PORSCHE 1950, a reference to the Lohner-Porsche of 50 years before. Sadly, it was just after attending this show that the Professor suffered his stroke. Had he survived, a mere two months later he might have attended a little ceremony to mark the production of the 500th German-built car on 21 March 1951.

It was at another show, at Frankfurt, in 1951, that a number of alterations were announced, such as tubular shock absorbers and hydraulic brakes, but the biggest change was a larger engine, of 1300 (in fact 1286cc) capacity from an increase in bore to 80mm. With the increase came radical new cylinders – they were made from aluminum but the usual iron liner required with this material was deleted, the bores being chrome-plated instead. The 1300, with a compression ratio of 6.5:1

Below: The 356 Super 90 was so named because of the output of the engine – 90bhp.

so that it could run on pump fuel, gave 44bhp at 4200rpm. This was not much more than the 1100, but it gave it in a much more relaxed manner.

The big-engine news, though, was reserved for Paris in October. On display on the Porsche stand was one of the Gmünd coupés, still looking somewhat the worse for wear. It had been hammered around the bankings at Monthléry, an oval racetrack near Paris, for 72 hours at an average speed of 94.66mph, in spite of the loss of top gear, setting a whole clutch of new world records in the process. Nestling in the tail of the car was an even bigger engine, a 1500.

Since an increase in bore was not possible – the Mahle chrome-plated aluminum cylinders were on the limit – a longer stroke was needed. This meant an increase in the throw of the cranks but then there was the problem that the big-end bolts would contact the camshaft, placed directly beneath the crankshaft. The solution was compact but complex: a roller-bearing crankshaft, made by Hirth. If it was at all abused – which meant if it was not scrupulously maintained – it tended to fail,

often spectacularly and always expensively. I have had a chance to inspect one of these assemblies at first hand, and they are beautifully engineered right down to the radial serrations or teeth on the journals but they are also not the sort of thing that can be slung into an engine on an assembly line any-old-how. Cost, and its poor reputation, prevented the Hirth roller-bearing crank becoming widespread in road cars, although it did become popular for competition work. However, the spatial problems of the big-end bolts were eventually overcome by a new design of connecting rod, and in September 1952 a plain-bearing 1500 engine was offered, giving 55bhp at 4400rpm. With its softer camshaft, lower compression ratio and smaller carburetors, this model soon became known as the *Damen*, or lady, because of its flexibility and lack of fuss. The roller-bearing version, called the Super, gave 70bhp at 5000rpm but was capable of considerably more in racing tune – in fact, 70bhp was invariably the minimum output since Porsche power figures usually erred on the conservative side.

Below: One of the rarer 356s, a Hardtop, on display at Earl's Court Motor Show, London, 1961.

Left: The Type 547 quad-cam engine was a tight fit in the 356's tail, but the result was one of the all-time great Porsches, the immortal Carrera.

Development was continuous and modifications were introduced as and when. Thus in mid-1952 there was a minor body change in that the body swept down and under the bumpers fore and aft, the bumpers themselves being moved outward, and a one-piece windshield (though still veed) appeared. By this time, too, it was obvious that the standard VW gearbox, designed for the Beetle's rather puny output, was overtaxed in the Porsche. Porsche had already designed a new unit for VW, incorporating their own patented baulk-ring synchromesh. VW did not adopt it, so Porsche came to an arrangement with the gearbox manufacturers Getrag, who built it for them.

Meanwhile production had long outgrown the spare space in the Reutter plant: more was urgently called for. An area behind Reutter's was available but the cash for it was not. The outbreak of the Korean War had seen the Americans retain the Spitalwaldstrasse premises and they would not be returned until 1955. The cash for the new factory did appear, however, and from a rather unexpected source – Studebaker, in America. This came about through the efforts of the man who put Porsche on the map in America, Max Hoffman.

Hoffman was an Austrian, having been born in Vienna in 1904. He had emigrated to America. He was known to the Porsches for Anton Piëch had been his lawyer. An astute businessman and sports-car fanatic, he had foreseen the rising popularity of European two-seaters in the United states, and sold many famous marques such as Mercedes-Benz and Jaguar from his plush Park Avenue showrooms in New York. Always on the lookout for new sales, he took delivery of three 1100s in late 1950, two of which were promptly bought by another arch-enthusiast, Briggs Cunningham. At the time Ferry Porsche envisaged sales of no more than 500 cars worldwide and suggested to Hoffman that he could sell perhaps five a year in the United States. Hoffman's reply was a classic: 'I'm not interested unless I can sell that many per week!' By 1954 he was taking 30 percent of Porsche's output, setting a trend that has never stopped. It was Hoffman who introduced the men from South Bend to the folks from Stuttgart, and in May 1952 a contract to design and build the prototypes of a new car were signed. This brought in some $500,000, enough to go ahead with the new plant. Assembly began in late 1952 in Porsche's new home.

Hoffman was also responsible for a curious, and little-known Porsche, the America Roadster. This was intended to make use of the 1500 Super engine on the track, and was, in effect, a lightened, open 356 two-seater. The body was slightly more conventional than the other models, in that there were fully open rear wheel-arches and a fender line that rose over the rear wheels, while it was made out of aluminum by Glaser of Ullërsricht. It is not clear exactly how many America Roadsters were made but they soon earned a formidable reputation on the race tracks of America driven by names such as John and Josie von Neumann, Briggs Cunningham, John Bentley, Phil Walters and Bill Lloyd.

The America Roadsters were built in 1952, and even then were not cheap, costing $4600. As Porsche sales grew Hoffman started pressing those in Germany for a downmarket, cheaper Porsche to compete with the newcomers from Britain, the Austin-Healeys, MGs and Triumphs. The result was one of the most charismatic Porsches ever, if one of the ugliest – the Speedster.

Introduced in 1954, the Speedster was based on the cabriolet but there the resemblance ended. It was very much a two-seater, like the America from which it was derived, with a flimsy top and a tiny little windshield, chrome-framed. With the top up, vision out is near enough nil. The overall shape is often referred to as an inverted bathtub in polite circles. Whatever you want to call it, there is no denying that it is a hilariously dumpy, squat, beetle-browed pudding bowl on four wheels. And yet, there is something purposeful about it, like a bulldog stomping undeflectably on its way, or a bug scampering across a slippery floor.

Reutter, who built the bodies on Cabrio chassis, in effect stripped them out. The seats were lightweight, interior trim minimal, the dashboard plain and bare. Because of all this, the Speedster was some 150 lb lighter than other Porsches and quite a bit cheaper. The latter was a bonus to those who bought it since, with its added lightness, it did not take enthusiasts long to realize that the Speedster

Below: The first two prototypes, with the mid-engined roadster in the background and the rear-engined coupé to the fore.

Above: Discretion was the name of the game with the Carrera – this simple badge is the only indication that the Type 547 engine nestles under the hood.

was one very quick machine and could annihilate anything else of equal engine capacity (and often machines with much bigger engines) on the track. In 1955 a certain Bengt Soderstrom won the Sports Car Club of America's Class F Production Championship. Up to 1500ccs, the Speedster was top dog.

Reverting to the main-stream models, 1955 saw a thorough reworking of the 356, enough to give it a new designation when it appeared at the Frankfurt Show in September of that year. Immediate identification of the model came from a new, curved windshield, though rubbing strips along the bottom of the body were less obvious. Of more significance, though, was what had happened in the tail. Gone was the 1100 engine, to disappear forever. The 1300 and 1300S (with roller bearings and giving 60bhp) were retained but the big news was that the 1500 had grown to 1600cc, thanks in part to a new three-piece crankcase. The *Damen* version with plain bearings gave 60bhp, the S with rollers 75bhp, not a vast increase over the 1500 but the advantages came in smoothness and tractability. There were suspension changes, too. Wheel sizes came down from 17 inches to 15 inches, springs were softened but dampers made firmer, there was an antiroll bar, and the steering was altered to reduce oversteer. There was also a new dashboard, and interior trim was improved.

It was in a 356A 1600 *Damen*, belonging to the British racing driver Nick Faure, that I had my introduction to 356 motoring, and driving one 30 years after it was built was quite an eye-opener. For a start it was surprisingly civilized for a 1950s sports car. Compared to something like an Austin-Healey or a Triumph TR – and especially an MG – it is incredibly refined. It absorbs bumps that would have the British cars leaping and jumping around. At speeds over 80mph, too, you know you are travelling quickly in the others from all the sound and fury around you: in the Porsche you are at a natural, comfortable, quiet cruising speed. The gearchange is superb, light and easy, but with that curious slightly rubbery feeling that comes with Porsche synchromesh.

Handling at normal speeds is also a revelation, the steering proving to be light yet direct with plenty of feel to it. But, if there is one facet of the car which creates more controversy than any other (looks apart) it is the handling *in extremis*. Primitive swing axles plus an engine in the tail add up to oversteer, no matter how you look at it (which is why, in later models, Porsche kept

You have to look closely to see the Carrera script on the fender of this 356A.

adding understeer to the chagrin of true *aficionados*). There is even a phrase to describe the handling of the early models: *wischen*, the German for wiping, a graphic description of the car's cornering attitudes. It was counteracted by *sagen*, or sawing, which is what the driver had to do to the steering wheel to stop ends swapping. If you did overstep the mark, you performed what Denis Jenkinson (Jenks of *Motor Sport* magazine), an archenthusiast of the early 356s if ever there was one, calls the 'ground-level flick-roll,' to the detriment of car and driver. The world, though, is

divided into two species: those who reveled in such antics (flick-roll apart, perhaps) and those who were frightened by them. What was often misunderstood was that the speeds at which a 356 became uncontrollable were usually considerably higher than those at which more conventional machines would long since have exited stage left. *Wischen* then just hopin' was not the way to conduct a 356.

Shortly after driving the 356A I had a chance to drive a 1957 356A Speedster belonging to an old friend, Del Mallet. Believe it or not, this car (reputed to have been bought new by Gloria Swanson) is used daily by Del to commute from his home on the outskirts of London to the center, a task which it carries out with considerable aplomb and utter reliability. The Speedster once more shows up that indefinable something about a Porsche from the 1950s that cannot be bottled and duplicated. There is a delicacy, a precision, a lightness of controls that is unique. The steering by modern standards is low-geared but it is also beautifully light and precise, the gearchange merely requires two fingers to flick it through the gate, and the clutch is smooth and well cushioned. The engine, too, responds instantly to the throttle, so it is easy to see why drivers took to the Speedster so readily. Treat it with finesse and it behaves like a thoroughbred horse, almost reading your mind in its reactions. What was rather surprising about this car was the amount of understeer when powering out of a corner. Still, this was preferable to arriving into the corner too quickly and finding out about *wischen*ing all over again. To cap it all, there is that other traditional Porsche feel of quality about the car, taut, solid and rattle-free.

(Interestingly, the 'ugly-duckling' Speedster has been highly flattered in the last few years by the appearance of replica Speedsters based on VW mechanicals. Though the paper specifications are similar, in practice the two cars are a million miles apart. Having driven a replica, all I can say is that you cannot beat the real thing.)

However, that same Frankfurt Show in 1955 which saw the appearance of the 356A also saw the launch of one of the most charismatic 356s ever, and one of the world's truly great sports racing cars, the 356 Carrera. This was a marriage between the 356 shell and underpinnings and an engine, coded in-house the Type 547, that had first been seen publicly in 1953. Fitted into a 550 Spyder, one of these engines had not only walked away with its class in the tough 1954 Carrera Panamericana, but came home third overall, a sensational result. Porsche was absolutely entitled to name a car after the event.

The engine, designed by Ernst Fuhrmann, who had cut his teeth on the Cisitalia Grand Prix car, and after whom a demon camshaft for racing was named, was a masterpiece of complexity. Quite apart from a roller-bearing crankshaft and twin plugs per cylinder, there was a convoluted network of shafts and spiral bevel gears to drive the camshafts, of which there were four, two per bank of cylinders.

The 356 Carrera had one of the most distinguished racing careers of any Porsche. Initial models had a capacity of 1498cc and gave 100bhp, though engine weight plus that of the dry-sump oil system and fatter tires added some 100 lb to the tail of the coupé, which helped to give better grip at the rear (or so it was said – what it did to the tail if it was lost in a corner can be imagined). Top speed was tantalizingly close to the magic 200kph (125mph).

The 10,000th Porsche – a coupé – rolled off the Zuffenhausen assembly on 16 March 1956, while the 1958 model range, introduced as usual at the Frankfurt Show in September, saw the 1300 engine and the Hirth roller-bearing crankshafts disappear. Diaphragm clutches first appeared this year too, while one rather unwelcome modification was the routing of the exhaust pipes through the bottom of the overriders to give better ramp clearance. All they did, though, was blacken the overriders and cause rapid rust. Porsche do make mistakes sometimes. Clutch and gearchange also came in for attention.

Another new model which joined the lineup in 1958 was the Hardtop. As its name implies, this was a removable affair for the cabriolet, giving open-topped motoring in the summer and the comfort of a saloon in winter. Some later versions had the hardtop welded permanently in position giving a 356 with a quite distinctive profile. The year 1958 also saw the 'ugly duckling' Speedster replaced by the more attractive Speedster D, D standing for Drauz, the coach-builder responsible for the body. However, such was the outcry from the Speedster purists that this was almost instantly changed to Convertible D to allow the Speedster fans their one-upmanship. Just to confuse matters,

some of the bodies for this model were supplied by the Belgian firm of D'Ieteren, and the name was changed later still to Roadster.

The Frankfurt Show of 1959 saw what was, perhaps, the most startling visual change to the 356. The whole nose of the car was raised and was fronted by a pretty massive bumper: a genuine 'face-lift.' The rear bumper was raised as well. Enter the 356B. Along with the new face came the invariable multitude of smaller modifications, most hidden, like the improved synchromesh, others slightly more obvious, such as more rear-seat room thanks to altered gearbox mountings.

By 1960 rationalization had taken place. The only engine options from 1960 onward were 1600s (apart from the Carrera) but there was a third option, the Super 90, to go with the Normal (60bhp) and Super (75bhp) versions. With typical Teutonic logic, it was so named because it gave near enough 90bhp, sufficient to propel the coupé to a maximum of 115mph, and even the less-aerodynamic Roadster to 110mph. Cornering with the Super 90 was improved by the use of a compensating spring at the rear which acted in the opposite way to an antiroll bar. Consisting of a single, wide-leaf spring attached to the hub either side, it reduced the roll stiffness and forced the front suspension to work harder and thus increase understeer.

In 1961 the basic 356 bodyshell was given its last major modifications. The windshield and rear window were enlarged, and more space was found under the hood at the front which also featured a squared-off lower edge. September of the same year also saw the 2-liter version of the Carrera, called the Carrera 2.

The late 1950s and early 1960s were the golden years of the 356, but as early as 1962 Porsche was heavily involved in the 356's replacement, the 901

Right: The dashboard of the Super 90 was neat and clean, with highly readable instruments and a biggish steering wheel by current standards.

Right: Natural habitat – a 356 Carrera running free in a test day at Donington during one of the Porsche Owner's Club open days.

Left: The Nürburgring, 1960: the Porsche wouldn't have won overall against Ferrari opposition no matter how battered – but you can bet it won its class. . . .

(later 911), and the days of the 356 were coming to an end. But not before one final fling: in 1963, at the now-traditional Frankfurt Show, the 356C was announced. To look at there was little difference between the 356B and C, for the 356B body was carried over, but the wheels now hid disk brakes, adopted at long last by Porsche, made by ATE to Dunlop patents. The range too was simplified, with just three engine options. The 1600 Normal engine was dropped, leaving the 1600S or Super 75, the 1600SC (replacing the Super 90) and the Carrera 2. With the 901 in the offing, by 1963 Porsche needed more control over their body-building side, and that year acquired the coach-building part of Reutter, naturally including the factory in which the whole of the German operation had started. (Reutter was renamed Recaro, and went on to fame the second time around as seat manufacturers).

The last 356 rolled off the Zuffenhausen assembly line in September 1963. A white cabriolet, it was the 76,303rd of the model, made up of 7,627 356s, 21,045 356As, 30,963 356Bs, and 16,668 356Cs. Well, not quite: ten more were built 'to special order.' Some people just couldn't bear to see the famed 356 disappear . . .

THE 911:
SUCCESS UNLIMITED

The Porsche 911 really is the most amazing car. At the time of writing it is celebrating its 21st birthday and seems to be at its absolute peak of mental and physical fitness. It has already achieved 'classic' status, usually reserved for machines long since out of production. The engine has grown from a 130bhp 2-liter to a 300bhp 3.3-liter *mit kompressor* but that is just the road version. It has won, in one form or another, every major competition event for which it was eligible from the Monte Carlo Rally to Le Mans. It has a mechanical layout that was not very fashionable when it was introduced, and is now regarded as thoroughly obsolete (but 911 owners blithely go their own way, enjoying themselves). It has been killed off by the pundits more times than most of them have had hot dinners but it is still alive and kicking. It has been called a triumph of development over design, arguably the most accurate statement ever made about it. It is one of the ultimate sports cars of all time.

By the late 1950s the 356 had grown a little middle-aged. It had started life as a light, rorty, spartan device, more for fun than practicality. Over the years it had been refined and improved, just like its owners who had grown out of the 'boy-racer' stage and wanted something more civilized. In this the 356 served them well, but new first-time owners dared to criticize the lack of

Previous pages: The 1973 911 Carrera set new standards in both power and looks.

Above: Butzi Porsche, grandson of Ferdinand, and a model of the 911.

Above: A prototype 911 when it was still called the 901, as seen on the license plate.

Left: Predecessor of the 911 was this prototype, the Type 695, designed when Porsche were thinking along four-seater lines.

Below: A divergence of models – the S on the left is kitted out with the famous five-spoke forged alloy wheels, the cheaper T on the right with plain steel ones.

luggage space, the noise and the handling. A new model, better-looking, more spacious, quieter, with better road manners was the logical step to take. However, to follow up a success is not always easy.

What to make? Initial thinking went along four-seater lines. This led to a prototype, the Type 695. By this time the third generation of Porsches was working in the company, and it was Ferry's eldest, Ferdinand Alexander (nicknamed Butzi) who was in charge of the styling studio. For the 695, which was on a wheelbase almost a foot longer than the 356, Butzi designed a stylish and elegant shape. The nose of the car, the 'face' as Butzi called it, was recognizably Porsche, in that there were the traditional sloped-back headlights, like those of the 356B and C, and no large air intake. Compared to the 356, however, the front was much cleaner and

smoother. The fender line was a gentle, subtle curve, sweeping back from the headlamps to blend smoothly into the tail. The top, however, was like no Porsche before: instead of the typical beetle-backed hump it was mostly glass, with a thin, almost flat roof, and the rear dropped sleekly down to the tail, giving a semi-fastback line.

Since the new car was both bigger and more upmarket, a new engine would obviously be required. It would have to have the sort of performance that the twin-cam four in the Carrera gave but without the attendant fuss, noise and servicing problems. A six-cylinder engine emerged as the most promising. Of course, it would be air-cooled, and of course it would be a boxer (horizontally opposed): nothing else was considered. A couple of variations on a theme was tried, one of which looked promising. This featured two camshafts,

An early S with short wheelbase, those forged alloy wheels and very period Porsche logo down the side.

one above and one below the crankshaft, operating the valves via pushrods. The carburetors were placed outboard of the heads, and fed the air/fuel mixture into the cylinders through porting that threaded its way between the valves. It gave 120bhp at 6500rpm, but had two drawbacks that soon emerged. The first was that a push-rod layout limited the development of power, particularly for racing, the second was that it was very wide.

Since this engine used two camshafts anyway, it was obvious that the only sensible thing to do was put them in the heads, thus creating a single ohc design. The carburetors were placed in a logical position too, directly above the heads, where the mixture could almost fall into the cylinders. By the time the revised six was being taken seriously, it was in the hands of yet another third-generation Porsche, Ferdinand Piëch, Louise's eldest. Of all the Porsches and Piëchs, he was the one who showed most of his grandfather's technical brilliance: after going on to greater things within the Porsche organization, culminating in the mighty 917s, he would move across to VW where he would become known as the father and champion of four-wheel-drive for high performance cars: the Audi quattro is his.

As with the 356, the new engine's cylinders were separate finned affairs capped by the one-piece heads. Other features included a remarkably stiff crankshaft, near-hemispherical combustion chambers, an axial, as distinct from a radial, fan, and dry-sump lubrication, as much to get sufficient quantities of oil to circulate as anything else, since oil acts as a coolant in air-cooled engines. With a 9.0:1 compression ratio, this engine,

project number 901, developed 130bhp at 6100rpm, and 129lb ft of torque at a highish 4200rpm. From the outset it was a screamer not a slogger.

However, by 1962 a fundamental rethink had taken place about the concept of the car. Four-seaters were not really Porsche domain: such a car would not be protected by being in a niche of its own as the 356 was in being virtually Germany's only sports car. It would be up against the likes of the Mercedes-Benz coupés. So the decision was taken to make the new car, the 901 following the engine type number, into a straightforward 2+2, the usual nomenclature for a two seater with occasional (very occasional) seats behind. A new wheelbase was chosen, only some 4 inches longer than that of the 356.

For the 901 Butzi kept the nose of the 695 from the A-post forward, but modified the rest. The most radical change was to the roof: no longer was it a semifastback, it was a pure fastback, and the line Butzi chose was a masterpiece. Smooth, clean, lithe, it is one of the constants in the 911's life story, an instant recognition point.

With the dimensions chosen, work started on the chassis. Kommenda, in charge, at first would not have anything to do with the 2+2 design but a threat from Ferry to farm the work out to Reutter brought him back into line. The resulting sub-structure was similar to that of the well-proven 356s. However, given a clean sheet of paper, as the Porsche engineers were, the suspension came in for considerable discussion. One of the imperatives for the new car was that it had to have more luggage space up front. The traditional

transverse torsion-bar arrangement of the VW and the 356 took up too much space. Possible alternatives included double wishbones or Mac-Pherson struts, introduced by Ford in the early 1950s, and which were gaining growing acceptance. The latter setup was chosen, since it meant only one (lower) wishbone and the strut tops could be kept far apart for maximum space in between. Longitudinal torsion bars, operated by the lower wishbone, also took up no luggage space. On the whole, it was a neat, simple solution. At the back the 356's swing axle was deemed adequate, but a late change saw a switch from a pure swing axle to a semitrailing layout. The arms were in two parts, one angled and attached to the chassis at one end and the wheel hub at the other to give location, the other made of spring steel, acting as a pure trailing arm but capable of twisting so that it could flex and thus accommodate wheel angle changes: this latter arm operated the transverse torsion-bar springs. Up front again, steering was made rack and pinion, there was a five-speed gearbox, and brakes were disks all round.

All this, then, was the specification of the 901 when it was first shown in public at the usual Frankfurt Show in September 1963. However, Porsche made no secret of the fact that the car on display was very much a prototype and that production was a year away. Thus late 1963 and a large part of 1964 were taken up with the myriad of things necessary for cars to roll off an assembly line, so it was not until the Paris Show in 1964 that Porsche announced that they were ready to make 911s. And the company promptly hit a snag: Peugeot objected to the name. They had copyright in France on all three-digit numbers with a zero in the middle (as in 204, 305, etc). Fortunately 901 had not had time to become a recognized brand name so Porsche changed it to 911, though many parts were to bear a 90- prefix for many years to come.

The 911 started life on the production lines alongside its sister, the 356, but the latter was soon phased out. However, the Porsche people just cannot stop tinkering, and from then until today changes, modifications, variations, introductions, deletions and refinements have continually poured out of the design studios at Zuffenhausen.

Among the first to test a 911 (in fact, it was a pre-production 901 in early 1964) was the German magazine *Auto Motor und Sport*. They recorded a maximum speed of 131mph, and a 0-100kph (62.5mph) time of 8.7 seconds, both remarkable for a 2-liter. However, life in the first couple of years of the 911 was not all rosy. Those first cars suffered some awful defects – handling was one. With fairly skinny tires (165HR15s), intended to compensate for camber changes, a heavier than expected engine, and the problems associated with MacPherson struts when you do not know all that much about them, together with the weight of the engine on the back, the handling tended to be skittish, varying from strong understeer to rather sudden oversteer. Straight-line stability was not its

Above: This may look like an ordinary 911 but in fact is one of the rarest of them all, an ultra-lightweight 911R on non-standard wheels.

Below: Spot the difference? Probably not, but this is, in fact, a four-cylinder Type 912.

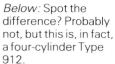

Left: Porsche driver extraordinaire, Vic Elford, in Porsche UK's demonstrator-cum-racer, GVB 911D.

strong point either, and the more sensitive drivers noted a variation in handling depending on the direction of turn. These were partly cured by a secret method: lumps of lead were hidden behind the corners of the bumpers, thus affecting both polar moment of inertia and weight distribution. It would take a while, involving wider tires, a longer wheelbase, and aerodynamic aids, before the road holding and handling would be *au point.* Meanwhile, the more daring drivers enjoyed themselves: the more timid didn't. It must be said, however, that simply from the layout of the car (with the engine slung out the back) even today a 911 will, on the limit, bring its tail around pretty quickly. If you are not sharp on the uptake (sometimes even if you are), excessive speed in a corner can mean a backward investigation of the flora and fauna. But then, as with the 356, you would have to be travelling at a pace which would probably have seen any other car off as well. Another complaint was of flat spots in the carburetion, cured by a switch from Solex to Weber carburetors early in 1966.

The first 911 variant appeared in August 1966. With cam and porting changes plus a higher compression ratio, the output of the engine took a jump to 160bhp. The model in which it was fitted was called the 911S; other changes included ventilation for the brake disks, and, for the first time,

forged magnesium wheels with a five-spoke pattern that was to become famous. Their rim width was increased to 5J over the standard steel items, not a vast amount, and they cost quite a bit more, but they were lighter (with beneficial effect on the sprung/unsprung weight ratio) and allowed more air to circulate around the brakes.

A rather more important development was announced at the same time. Right from the beginning of Porsche there had been an open version, and the Cabrios, Speedsters and Roadsters in the 356 range had made up a large proportion of its sales. Thus a drop-head, or open, 911 was pretty

Above: When it looked as if convertibles would be doomed by impending safety legislation, Butzi created this semi-convertible and another classic Porsche, the Targa, was born.

By 1970 the 911 had a 2-inch longer wheelbase, but so skilfully was it done that it was barely noticeable.

important. However, the rise of Naderism in America seemed to spell the end of the traditional convertible, since it did not look as if they would withstand the impending roll-over regulations. Butzi and the others considered the matter. Roll-over hoops had been mandatory in motor racing for some time, proving reasonably effective: could something similar be adapted to the 911 if the roof was removed? It probably could, and there might even be a bonus: it could act as strengthening, always lost from a monocoque when the top is chopped off. Instead of trying to disguise it Butzi made a feature out of it: he made it stand out both by its size and by the fact that it had a polished finish. The open section between windshield and hoop could be filled in with a collapsible panel, while the rear window was made of plastic and could be zipped in and out. Thus the new model was not strictly a convertible but it did give the 'wind-in-the-hair' enthusiasts more or less what they wanted. In fact, few ever seemed to unzip the rear window and in 1968 fixed glass was fitted instead. The new model was called the Targa, after another famous race in which Porsche racers had starred. Now this layout is called a 'targa top.'

Press reaction to the 911, once it became available other than in Germany, was fairly predictable. *Road and Track* tested one in March 1965. They said that 'The overall impression is that this car was built by men who know something about fast motoring and that it is destined for owners who feel the same.' They did not like the noise it made though, commenting that 'the engine, and in particular the cooling fan, remain much too audible,' the gearchange, a flat spot at about 2800rpm (this car was on Solexes) and the fuel consumption, but found the car 'perfectly controllable' – no handling problems here, that would only really appear in hindsight. Their summing-up is typical of almost every Porsche road test: 'Because the basic qualities are far above average, it undoubtedly rates in the top class among modern GT cars.' Jenks wrote in *Motor Sport* that it was 'The best car Porsche have yet built for road use' and that it was 'One of the best cars I've ever driven'. My predecessor on *Autosport*, John Bolster, reporting on the same car that Jenks had driven, recorded a top speed of 131mph, and a 0-60mph time of 8.7 seconds. His impressions of the car were succinctly summed up: 'Enjoyment, that's the word!' In fact, most

a standard four-speed box joined to the engine by both a torque converter and a clutch which were operated by a switch in the gear-lever knob. Thus the driver changed gear normally except that he did not have to use his left foot to depress the clutch (and he also rapidly learned not to rest his hand on the gear-lever knob too). The Sportomatic achieved some popularity but was neither really one thing nor the other, and was eventually dropped.

Changes started to come in fairly rapidly in the late 1960s. August 1968, for example, saw an important modification: a wheelbase longer by 2 inches. For this, designed to give a slightly more equitable balance, the wheels (and wheel-arches too) were moved backward the necessary amount, the rest staying where it was. Longer semitrailing arms were necessary, as were half shafts incorporating constant velocity joints to accommodate the greater angles in the shafts. Weight was removed from the tail by making the crankcase out of magnesium instead of aluminum, and the twin batteries were moved into the nose for the same reason. The S was fitted with even wider wheels, reducing understeer at low speeds and oversteer at high.

At about this time emission regulations began to come into force in America. To counteract the effects of this, and thus prevent too much power loss through the ungainly and inefficient equipment required, 1969 saw Bosch mechanical fuel injection fitted to the model for the first time. This not only helped on the emission front but gave an increase in output by 10bhp on both the L and the S to which it was fitted: the L then became the E, while the T stayed more or less the same. Boge self-levelling struts were tried on the E for a time in an attempt to obtain a better ride, but their effect was questionable and they were eventually dropped.

Another major change to the engine came the next year, when (via an increase in bore to 84mm) the capacity was upped for the first of many times to 2195cc. Though most owners reveled in the revability of the 2-liter, bottom-end punch was lacking, which could be a chore involving much gear changing in stop-start traffic. This put the power up to 125, 155 and 180bhp respectively for the T, E and S, but more significantly torque was improved as well. The T's rose from 116 to 130lb ft, the E's from 130 to 141lb ft, and the S's from 134 to 147lb ft, though the revs at which these figures were achieved were still pretty high – 5200rpm in the case of the S.

The evolution of the 911 continued, the next major change being yet another increase in capacity to 2341cc (the 2.4-liter model as it was called). The design of the cylinders as they were then meant that they could not be bored out without detrimental effects, so the extra capacity came from a longer stroke, 70.4mm instead of 66mm. However, in order to enable all models to run on regular grade (91 octane) fuel, the compression

testers raved about the road manners, which goes to prove that you had to be trying very hard indeed to discover the limits of its dynamic envelope – or be driving under slippery conditions. The august and respected *Autocar*, whose road tests are carried out by a team of drivers and take quite a while to conduct, added a word of caution, however, when they tested a 911S in late 1966:

> *The 911S is not a car for the novice and even the experienced fast driver must slow down when the roads turn wet. . . . In dry the adhesion is nothing short of phenomenal . . . (but) in the wet the power available is too much. . . . One needs to feed the throttle open progressively and carefully to prevent the tail twitching about, and to treat polished surfaces in town with discretion.*

In 1967 the original O series was replaced by the A series, the most significant changes being marginally wider wheels and a new model, the 911T, basically a downmarket, cheaper car with a 110bhp engine. The plain 911 became the 911L, and the S continued. Another innovation was an automatic gearbox, though not the conventional three-speed-plus-torque-convertor type: Porsche's device, called the Sportomatic, consisted of

Above: A 911 Targa shell is trimmed ready to receive its mechanicals while (*inset right*) a 924 shell sits above its complete drive train before being united with it. Porsche standards are exemplified by the care and attention a crankshaft receives as it is built up (*right*).

ratio was reduced across the board as well. Nevertheless, power rose to 130bhp, 165bhp and 190bhp for the T, E and S models respectively, with a corresponding increase in torque as well (to 160lb ft in the case of the S). By now too the gearbox was near its limit, so a new one was brought out, instantly recognizable by the fact that fifth, not first, was now the dog-leg ratio, making town driving more pleasant. There are those who swear that the early box was the sweetest of them all, but the majority of drivers preferred the new setup. And, in 1971, something appeared for the first time in a production car. Learning from track experience, an air dam was fitted under the front bumper of the S. A hint of things to come . . .

But 1971 was a fairly disastrous year. Inflation was taking off, and the Dm-$ rate worsened, putting up the price of cars in the United States. Sales dropped, from 16,761 to 11,715. On top of that, the family itself was going through a crisis. The company was top-heavy with Porsches and Piëchs, one of whom headed each of the major departments. Apart from jostling for power, they were blocking the way for talented people below them. Ferry Porsche's solution was pretty drastic but it was suggested that if they agreed to remove themselves from the company, the shares would be split into ten (for Ferry, Louise, and each of their four children) which would bring them in a tidy income per annum. This was indeed agreed upon, and Ernst Fuhrmann, designer of the original Carrera engine, was brought back from the Goetze piston ring company to become technical director in place of Ferdinand Piëch and head of

the company. Heinz Branitzki became financial director, Helmuth Bott took over development, and Anatole Lapine, an American, ex-GM and Opel, took over from Butzi. I can't help admiring Tony Lapine, incidentally, if only because, for relaxation, he drives an utterly terrifying Meskowski sprint car in historic race meetings in a very Porsche manner, all arms and elbows and very sideways!

Apart from aerodynamics, racing was affecting the 911 in other ways. This was to result in one of the finest Porsches ever in 1972. It was intended originally as an 'homologation special' for Group 4 racing which called for a production run of 500 off. Hence the new model was first stripped of all non-essentials such as soundproofing and undercoating and even door trim. As it was a racing car too it had to be fitted with very fat tires, so the wheel-arches were heavily flared, particularly at the back. There were heavier antiroll bars fore and aft, and Bilstein dampers were standard. And, to give the car a better chance in the 3-liter class there was yet another increase in capacity, to

2687cc, via a bigger bore of 90mm. In order to accommodate this a new type of cylinder was used, which eliminated any inserts and relied on a nickel-silicon carbide coating on the aluminum cylinder walls. Other than that, though, the engine was pure 911S, and the output was up to 210bhp at 6300rpm. There was only one name it could carry, of course: Carrera.

The story of the 2.7 Carrera is quite amazing. The sales staff did not care for the idea of having to clear 500 racers. One suggestion was that senior members of the company who were entitled to a top-ranking car would be forced to take a Carrera. Unfortunately for the management this was not necessary because within a week of the car being displayed at Paris in October 1972, all 500 were sold. In fact, so high was the demand that production continued: by April 1973 the 1000th had been built which meant the model could be homologated into Group 3. In all some 1600 Carreras were made, of which roughly 600 were kitted out with standard 911S interior trim. There were also 49 RSR versions, pure racers.

Visually, the Carrera was something else again. In the initial run they were all white with red or blue swirling Carrera logos down the side – this was one car you could not miss. In addition, building on experience with aerodynamics, a curious appendage sprouted out of the engine cover: due to its shape it was called a *bürzel*, or duck's tail. Whatever you called it, it was effective, reducing tail-end lift from a nasty 320 lb at maximum speed to a much more reasonable 93 lb. This was doubly useful since the performance – from an unblown 2.7-liter car, remember – was staggering: a top speed of 150mph and a 0-60mph time of less than 6 seconds.

For the 1974 model year the 2.7-liter engine was standardized across the board, though in varying states of tune. The base model became just the 911 with 150bhp, the E became the S with 175bhp, and the Carrera topped the line, replacing the earlier S (somewhat confusingly) with 210bhp. In general, though, the cars for the United States were down in power compared to their European sisters, a reflection of the ever-tightening emission laws (the 1973/74 Carrera in the States only gave the same output as the European S, 175bhp).

American crash regulations were also responsible for what could have been a disaster visually had it not been treated with care and style by Tony Lapine and his department: 5mph bumpers. These were integrated so well into the overall design that, along with the flared arches and aerodynamic aids, the 911 was taking on a much more aggressive and masculine look. Some mourned the loss of the original's litheness, others welcomed the more gutsy image.

In 1974 the 2.7 Carrera was replaced by the Carrera RS 3.0. As its name implies, the engine capacity grew yet again, to 2993cc. This was another homologation special, but, since it was regarded as 'evolutionary,' the rules to qualify for Group 3 only required 100 to be made. In fact, Porsche made 109, of which about half were turned into full-blown racers.

Above: The two faces of the 911. For the road, the Targa: for the track the Carrera.

Below: This 1971 911T had an engine capacity of 2.2 liters.

Above: The ultimate unblown 911 to date is probably the Carrera RSR 3.0, seen here doing what it does best – cornering very hard.

Right: To comply with safety regulations, the rear spoilers on road-going 911s were rubber-edged, as seen on this 1975 Turbo.

The significant point about this model was that, to overcome cylinder-wall-thickness limitations, the crankcase reverted to a more rigid aluminum construction, with wider stud spacings and Nickasil-coated bores of 95mm diameter, later standardized across the range. There were also new head castings to take the new stud spacing, though manifolding, injection, ignition and camshafts were as on the 2.7-liter car – Porsche, in effect, detuned the racing RSR engine for road use. In this form for road use it gave 230bhp at 6200rpm, and 203lb ft of torque at 5000rpm. The suspension had the increased 'swing-axle effect' from the racers at the rear, and the car sat on Pirelli CN36s (215/60x15 at the front, 230/60x15 at the back), fitted to 8- and 9-inch wheels respectively. The brakes were from the 917 – 11.8 inches in diameter and 1.2 inches thick.

Visual identity came from an enormous opening for the oil cooler in the front spoiler, even wider flared wheel-arches, and a vast 'tea-tray' spoiler at the back: to comply with road regulations, Porsche supplied two of these with each car, one rubber-edged for normal use, the other solid for racing. To the *cognoscenti*, the Carrera RS 3.0 is probably the ultimate unblown Porsche, with its exhilarating top speed of 150mph, its wild looks and its great scarcity.

The 911 Turbo appeared in October 1974 and in 1975 it was followed by the Carrera 3, not to be confused with the RS 3.0. Despite the increase in capacity to 2994cc, peak power dropped slightly to 200bhp, but the whole unit was much more flexible and tractable. The chance was taken at the same time to simplify the range to consist of the Turbo, the 3 liter Carrera 3, and the 2.7-liter 911, the latter with 165bhp. By August 1975 all models received an antirust boost when body panels started being made of the same galvanized steel as the chassis.

The next round of major changes to the 911's specification came in 1977, following a couple of lean years due to the Yom Kippur War. The range was rationalized yet again, with both the Carrera 3 and the base 911 replaced by the 911SC. The engine was a detuned version of the Carrera 3, giving 180bhp, but performance remained about the same and flexibility was improved yet again. There was a Sport variant, with added aerodynamic appendages, fatter wheels, and uprated suspension. This was followed in 1980 by a rise in compression ratio to 9.8:1, and more power again, 204bhp this time.

The next major step came in 1981 at the almost inevitable Frankfurt Show. Porsche displayed a *studie*, a design exercise, which featured four-wheel-drive – and a fully opening top. The importance of this became obvious some six months later when the 911 Cabriolet was announced as a production model. With no roll-over hoop, it is a true convertible in the best Cabrio traditions. It was made possible when it was realized that the American roll-over regulations could be met with the standard windshield surround acting as a roll-over hoop. Like the Targa, you cannot get hold of a Turbo Cabrio – well, not from Porsche anyway – but it does give an additional, though rare, dimension to Porsche 911 motoring.

Above: Introduced in 1985, the 911 Turbo with the Sport Equipment package gave a street Turbo the 934 look with a sloping nose and pop-up headlamps.

Below: Porsche's contender for the Supercar stakes, the 911 Turbo is a blend of shattering performance yet total tractability.

The last real major round of revisions to the 911 range came in September 1982. Engine capacity increased yet again, to 3164cc, using the 74.4mm stroke from the Turbo. As usual this led to more power (231bhp at 5900rpm) and torque (209lb ft at 4800rpm) but with a claimed 10 percent better fuel consumption. At the same time all the un-blown 911s were named Carrera, which is the situation today. However, at the time of writing, Porsche have just announced that you can now order a Special Equipment model; this means you can get the normally aspirated 3.2-liter Carrera with the body, front and rear spoilers, and running gear from the Turbo – and on the Targa and Cabrio as well.

I have been lucky enough to drive a variety of 911s over the years and it has been fascinating to see how they have changed – or, in some instances, how they have stayed the same. The early cars, up to the 2.7-liter models, relied on revs to get their performance. It was as if, at about 3500-4000rpm, another pair of cylinders was switched in. Gradually the torque curve has been filled in, though, so now there is both power and torque at any revs. The constants include the steering, always light and direct and beautifully weighted, a gearchange that takes time to wear in, and an amazing feeling of solidity.

The last 911 I drove was a 1985 Carrera for an *Autosport* road test. To try and put across the flavor of the machine, I can but quote from my report at the time:

> *To say the 911 is all about performance is to state the absolute obvious – but what performance! What Car? managed a sensational 5.5secs to 60mph from a standstill, a mere 0.4secs slower than a Turbo! The same car then rocketed on to 100mph in 15.2secs, and 120mph in 22.6secs. Pors-che claim a top speed of 152mph and few will quibble with this – Porsche, unlike some manufacturers, tend to be rather conservative in their claims.*
>
> *And, subjectively, the performance feels and sounds as exhilarating, as spine-tingling, as the figures suggest. From the moment you switch on, when the engine will idle with that characteristic 'whoomph, whoomph' for a while, you know there's a beautifully made, jewel-like power house behind you. Nor is it all sound and fury, signifying nothing – though it must be said that in traffic jams there was an annoying unprogressiveness to the throttle. Floor it, however, and the muted growl from behind takes on a deeper bark, the exhaust at first over-powered by fan whine, but as revs increase the harsh beat from the exhaust takes over, building up to a crescendo at the red line (reached almost alarmingly quickly in first and second) that is without doubt one of the most joyous noises to issue from any car currently in production. Could this be one of the reasons 911 owners keep coming back for more?*
>
> *The 911 has a reputation for tricky handling at the limit. That may well be the case, but in some 400 miles of travel in the test car it never put a foot wrong. The steering has a feel to it that puts you back about 20 years when rear-engined cars were all the vogue: it is light yet direct and, thanks to a lack of assistance, has superb feel.*
>
> *Under 99 per cent of conditions the 911 displays mild understeer, changing to neutrality as power is applied. Deliberately entering a corner on a trailing throttle, or under braking, shows that the basic, unalterable dynamics of the 911 have been disguised but are still there: the tail starts to dictate the line through a corner. What has to be borne in mind is that in slippery conditions the*

Above: To celebrate a Le Mans win, a limited number of Turbos were finished in Martini colors – overall white with blue and red flashes.

However, I have to say that the 911 I enjoyed most was a toss-up between the 2.7 Carrera or the fabulous Carrera RS3.0. To drive, the RS3.0 is near perfection. Yes, it is noisy, but that glorious, unique growl from the flat six is music even to heathen ears. The acceleration is startling yet so smooth you have to check the speedometer to believe the speeds at which you are travelling. The 911s are tail-happy, but not the RS – there is so much rubber at the back that it sticks like glue, and even on a racetrack there is more understeer than oversteer (though I drove the road version). The steering is absolutely right and the brakes – wow!

There are two versions of the 911 that have not been mentioned yet, one very much downmarket, the other at the top end of the scale. The first is the 912, the second, of course, the Turbo.

The loss of the 356 in March 1965 meant that the cheapest Porsche was expensive. As a stopgap, until the 911 was fully established in its niche, Porsche produced the 912. This consisted of 911 body and running gear but with the 356C's 1600cc flat four in the tail. The 912 is surprisingly little known or mentioned – surprisingly, because in its first year of life it outsold the six-cylinder car, 6440 to the 911's 4865. It soldiered on until 1969, by which time well over 30,000 had been made, a useful addition to the sales figures. It was dropped to make way for the 914/4 and 916/6, but when the 914/4 came to the end of its life in 1975 it was reintroduced yet again, for one year only, and purely for the American market. Since the 356 power unit was long since out of production the 912 was fitted with the VW 2-liter flat four, almost identical to that of the 914/4, giving 90bhp at 4900rpm. A total of 2099 were made.

Back, though, to 1973. On the Porsche stand at Paris that year was a 911 with the full body works – flared arches, spoilers, the lot. And one odd thing: written into the swoopy paint flash down the side, and just discernible, was the word 'Turbo.' Of course, everyone assumed it was a dream car, a styling exercise. But at the same show exactly one year later on the Porsche stand was a production Turbo. It was project number Type 930 and was called that in-house, but the sales department called it the 911 Turbo. Porsche finally had a contender for the Supercar to end all Supercars.

As with the Carrera, it was intended to be an homologation special for a 'silhouette formula' for the Manufacturer's Championship to be introduced in 1976. This called, more or less, for an almost total lack of restrictions except that the basic shape should bear more than a passing resemblance to the production car on which it was based, and kept basically the same power unit in the same position.

Thus, to look at, the Turbo bore a close resemblance to the racing RSR. There was that deep front spoiler, fat wheel-arches filled with Pirelli CN36 rubber (185s at the front, 215s at the back) and, naturally, a massive rear spoiler. The same car provided the aluminum block and cylin-

oversteer comes in at much lower speeds. The problem lies in the difference between grip in the dry and in the wet, which is more marked than in other, more conventional, cars.

Obviously, for a car that requires a 'slow in, fast out' driving technique, brakes are important. Those on the 911 do all that is required of them: the only way we can see them being improved is the adoption of anti-lock braking.

Fat tyres and a stiff suspension setting are not the best way to achieve a smooth ride, and sure enough the 911 is not the best in this respect. Even on motorways there is some ripple, and potholes and roadworks can cause distinct thumps and jars. On the other hand it is far from soft and wallowy, a feature which many prefer.

Mind you, it was not all good news. I could not stand the clutch ('stupidly heavy and with an odd, over-center feel') or the gearchange ('The impression is that the synchromesh . . . is positively fighting engagement'), while the switchgear and, almost inevitably, the heating and ventilation came in for criticism. I summed up my feelings for the car when I said: 'I for one hope the 911 survives for a long time to come. It is unique, a car which inspires more loyalty and affection than any other . . . for all the right reasons.'

der dimensions, so the capacity was 2994cc. Since turbocharging in effect raises the compression ratio, this was dropped to 6.5:1.

The KKK turbocharger blew through Bosch K-Jetronic fuel injection (on later models the Bosch Motronic engine management system, much more sophisticated, would be used). Turbocharger lag, caused by compressor revs dropping when it has little work to do, such as on the overrun, and then having to accelerate up to working speeds again, was reduced to a minimum by a bypass in the intake which allowed incoming air to circulate round and back to the compressor, and thus keep it spinning. With a wastegate fitted to give a maximum boost pressure of 0.8 bar (12psi), the 930 Turbo engine produced a rousing 260bhp at 5500rpm, and a splendid 254lb ft of torque at 4000rpm. Mind you, it did need 97 octane fuel.

Other modifications over the standard 911 included a much beefier, four-speed gearbox, a bigger diameter clutch, heftier cast aluminum trailing arms at the rear, larger wheel bearings, and yet wider wheels, 7 inches at the front and 8 inches at the back, made of forged alloy. The bodywork at the back had to be strengthened as well, which is why there has never been a Targa or Cabrio Turbo. To cap it all, homologation special or not, the Turbo was fully trimmed to luxury levels. This was no thinly disguised racer, in fact,

but a genuine flagship, a Porsche Supercar.

The intention may have been to build 500 off for homologation purposes, but the Turbo took off like the 2.7 Carrera and others before it. In fact, 1300 were built in the first two years. In 1977 the Turbo was given another, and to date final, increase in capacity. Both bore and stroke were stretched this time, to give a capacity of 3299cc, which led (thanks in part to an intercooler as well) to 300bhp at 5500rpm, and torque flashed up to no less than 303lb ft at 4000rpm. There were the latest Pirelli P7s under the wheel-arches too, of 205 section at the front and 225 at the back. Tested by *Autocar*, the 3.3-liter Turbo recorded a maximum speed of 162mph, a 0-60mph time of a stunning 5.1 seconds, and an equally dramatic 50-70mph time of 2.2 seconds. Blink and you'll miss it . . .

To drive a Porsche turbo is one of the all-time great experiences. At first it can be a little daunting: the bodywork overflows the sides and is invisible, so you find you give yourself plenty of *lebensraum* all round you, especially in traffic. And you keep saying to yourself '300bhp, turbocharged' over and over again. But after a while an astonishing thing happens: it is as if the car shrinks. You expect low-speed engine temperament, poor town manners, a raucous power unit but you find that it is as docile as an ordinary family saloon, no drama, no fuss. Once you have grown a

Below: The car they didn't think could be made, but which eventually appeared in 1981: the 911 Cabriolet with fully opening roof.

little used to it, its character changes: when you find yourself a nice, clear, open road and press the loud pedal to the floor it simply takes off as if rocket propelled. Grip in the corners is phenomenal, and there is nothing more spine-tingling than powering a Turbo through a fast corner and feeling yourself flung sideways as if in some fairground device, g-forces trying to tear you out of your seat, but the seat itself and the belts holding you fast.

Then, after you have had your fun, you can potter back into town as coolly and as calmly as you like. That is the Turbo's greatest asset. Other supercars will give the same blinding performance, the same cornering powers, but few can match its utmost docility at the other extreme. The Turbo is the only practical Supercar.

Mind you, the Turbo is not the ultimate 911 for the road. That honor must go to the 959, announced in September 1983, as a *studie* for a Group B racer but which also 'contains all the prerequisites for everyday road use,' as the press release said.

The 959 was based on the Turbo in shape and technical concept but there any resemblance ends. The cockpit is visually 911 and the engine is a flat six in the tail, but the rest owes more to the 934. Take the engine, for example. It is a descendant of that used in the 935s and 936s, with a capacity of 2.85 liters (which corresponds to 4 liters when the turbo factor is taken into account). There are water-cooled, four-valve heads with

hydraulic valve adjustment and twin turbochargers and intercooler. Power output is 400bhp, enough to rocket this missile to 100kph (62.5mph) in 4.9 seconds and on up to a top speed of 186mph.

All this power is fed to the fat 17-inch-diameter wheels via a six-speed gearbox and an electronically controlled four-wheel-drive system which can vary the amount of power going to front or rear wheels either automatically or manually by the driver. The suspension follows racing practice too: gone are the 911's MacPherson struts and trailing arms, replaced by twin wishbones at each corner, controlled by twin shock absorbers and, at the front, twin coil springs. Adjustment of both ride height and spring rating is possible even while the car is on the move. Yet another novel feature is a tire-pressure monitor to warn of a puncture or a split in the magnesium wheels.

Externally the body has been considerably cleaned up. The headlamps stay in the top of the fenders, rather than down in the spoiler as on the 934, but they have been beautifully faired in. A small change that may not look very valuable, but is, is the removal of the rain gutter above the doors – they had a drag effect out of all proportion to their size. At the back the spoiler is a bridgelike affair, sweeping up and over the tail from one fender to the other. The nose is beautifully clean, and joining the flared wheelarches is a skirt that, in pre-war days, might well have been called a running board. All this has resulted in a drag factor of 0.32: not perhaps brilliant compared to something

further 20 pure competition cars for racing. Three versions are planned, a luxury car complete with full leather interior and air conditioning, a sports road-going car, and the aforementioned pure racer. The basic starting price will break the £100,000 ($140,000) barrier. What is more it will meet all future vehicle emission regulations as well.

Few cars reach the age of 21. That the 911 has not only done so, but, with the 959, in a way that puts it miles ahead of anything else in the field of technical innovation, must go to prove something. That famous triumph of development over design?

The trouble with the 911, as far as the historian is concerned, is that, the moment you write about it, whatever you have written is out of date. For example, Porsche have just announced the mid-1985 changes for the 1986 model year. The Sport Equipment versions of the Carrera have been mentioned: the Turbo has come in for similar treatment. There is a 30 percent uplift in power output, thanks to a higher profile camshaft, a bigger turbocharger and intercooler, and a modified exhaust system. At the rear there are wider, lower profile tires – 245/45VR16s, compared to 225/50VR16s – fitted to 9Jx16 forged alloy wheels (remember the first 911's puny 165HR15s?). The most striking change, though, comes to the bodywork. Taking a leaf from the customizers such as bb and Kamei, a special division within the factory has come up with a new kit which includes a very 934-like nose minus the tops of the fenders and with pop-up headlamps, while there are air-ducts in the rear wheel-arches. With the Special Equipment version of the Turbo, Porsche have made it look distinctly different from 'ordinary' 911s.

That's a brief rundown of the 911 story to date. But, as has been said, Porsche never leave things alone, so please don't shoot the author if, when you read this, you find it has been overtaken by events. The 911 is a living animal, constantly changing and improving. Long may it continue.

like the 0.30 of the Audi 200 saloon, but excellent compared to the brick-like figures associated with the 934. And, to keep weight down (the 959 weighs a mere 2485 lb) the body shell is made of a light but rigid Aramid composite material called Kevlar, while the hood and doors are made from aluminum.

Late in 1985 Porsche announced that the 959 would go into production with a minimum run of 200 at least to qualify for Group B, plus at least a

Below: Most cars have long since retired before they reach the age of 21. The 911 is not just still going strong, it is stronger than ever. In the form of the 959 it has four-wheel drive, 400bhp and a top speed of 186mph.

THE MID-ENGINE EXPERIMENT: THE 914

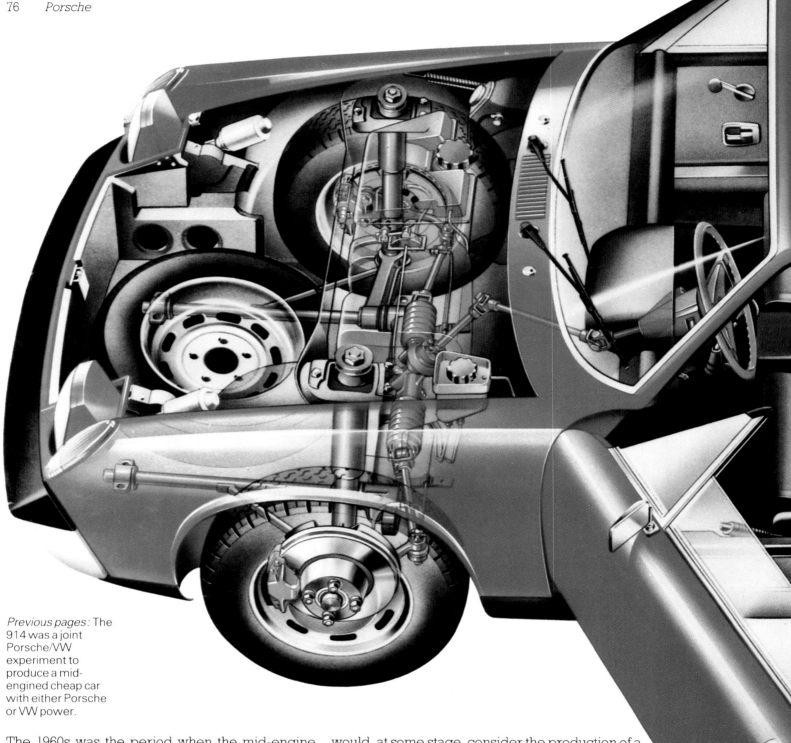

Previous pages: The 914 was a joint Porsche/VW experiment to produce a mid-engined cheap car with either Porsche or VW power.

The 1960s was the period when the mid-engine configuration finally came of age on the racetracks of the world. While Grand Prix racing had been the preserve of such cars since the late 1950s, it took until 1963 for a mid-engined machine to win Le Mans, and 1965 for the last bastion of a front-engined car, Indianapolis, to topple. Many manufacturers reasoned that, if the racing car of today is the sporting car of tomorrow, then mid-engined road cars had to be the way to go.

Porsche, of course, were very familiar with, and firmly committed to, such a layout for their track cars. Ever since the little 550 they had been successful with it, and, along with Cooper, could be said to be responsible for its ultimate takeover on the circuits.

Thus it was almost inevitable that Porsche would, at some stage, consider the production of a mid-engined road car, one which was nearer in concept if not detail to their racers. This would put the firm in the position of drawing more direct parallels between the successes of the cars on the track and the attributes of those on the road. However, the costs of going solo on such a venture would be formidable, so, not for the first or last time, Ferry turned to the spiritual ancestor of Porsche, VW. He approached Heinz Nordhoff with the suggestion that Porsche design a new sports car to carry both VW and Porsche names. The idea of the dynamic image of Porsche to try and update a staid and non-sporting VW range, even considering the Karmann Ghia, appealed to Nordhoff. He had a new model, the 411, on the stocks, and the new power plant from this car, an air-cooled

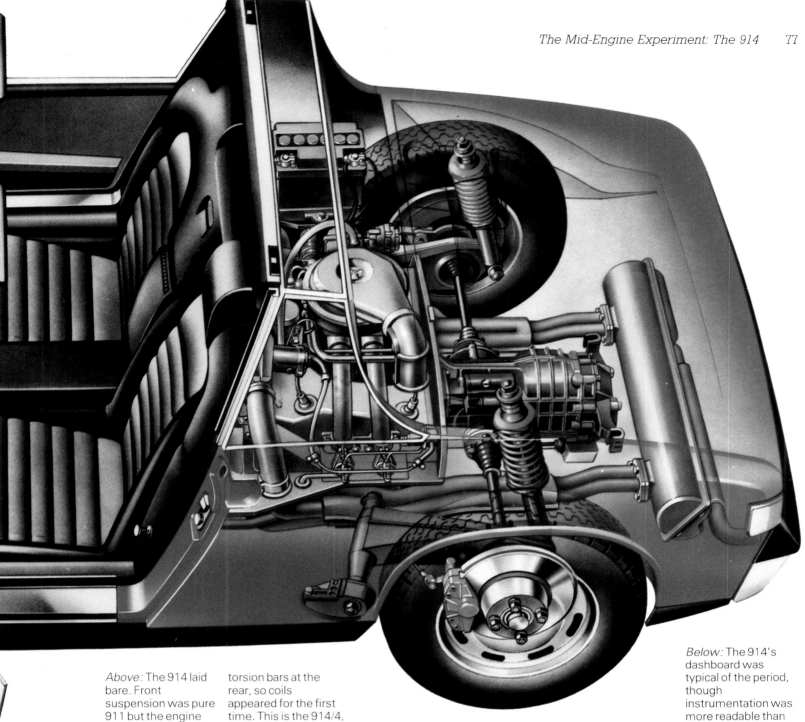

Above: The 914 laid bare. Front suspension was pure 911 but the engine location prevented torsion bars at the rear, so coils appeared for the first time. This is the 914/4, with VW power.

Below: The 914's dashboard was typical of the period, though instrumentation was more readable than average.

flat four, with a capacity of 1679cc, could be used.

The advantage to Porsche, of course, apart from cashing in on the racing image, was that it would give them a downmarket, cheaper car. Porsches had never been exactly cheap but over the years prices had risen to well out of the reach of the average enthusiast – the 911 was priced in Mercedes-Benz and Jaguar country. The new car, therefore, had three things going for it: cost, the backing of VW, and image. What could go wrong?

Quite a lot, in fact. The first problem was the original deal between two old friends, Ferry and Nordhoff. This was very much a handshake affair in which Porsche would be responsible for the development of the new car, and there was a gentleman's agreement that Porsche could use the basics of the car but fit it with their own engine to sell as a downmarket Porsche. However, in 1967

SPL 267X

Above: Pop-up headlamps and those heavy bumpers do nothing at all for the 914's looks.

Previous pages: The 914 was not the prettiest of Porsches, and was one of the few not to be styled in-house at Zuffenhausen. The forged alloy wheels indicate that this is a 914/6.

Nordhoff fell seriously ill, and his successor, Kurt Lotz, was a new-comer to VW. He read the small print in the agreement: VW had full and sole rights to the new car. If Porsche wanted it they would have to buy what they needed at full commercial rates. This turned out to be more than the 911 shells which Karmann were building for Porsche. The dream of the cheap Porsche began to fade. To resolve this and other political problems, a new marketing company, owned jointly by VW and Porsche, was set up. In America, Porsche handed over its sales to a new division of VW, called Porsche + Audi (Lotz wanted to sell Audis in the United States, and a tie-up with the established Porsche gave the cars credibility). In America the new car would be sold as a Porsche only: elsewhere it would be sold as a VW-Porsche. The trouble was, the VW-Porsche was neither one thing nor the other...

Another mistake, perhaps, was the deliberate decision not to make it look like a Porsche. To this end an outside firm of consultants, Gugelot Design at Neu-Elm, was employed. They had a considerable reputation in the design field, but for cameras, shavers and so on – not for cars. However, they had produced quite a stylish machine for the chemical company Bayer, used to demonstrate the applications of plastics for car bodies. This formed the basis of the new joint car. That prototype was quite dashing, but by the time the nose

had been raised to give more luggage space, hefty bumpers added fore and after, and the three-quarter pillars chopped in the interests of better vision, the original sleek looks had been lost. The final result was clean and functional but also rather boxy and bland. It was neither pretty nor, like the 356 Speedster, appealingly ugly.

However, there was no doubting the engineering of the new car, project number 914. This was pure Porsche. The body/chassis structure was exceptionally sturdy considering it had a Targa (removable) top, with deep boxed sills below the doors and a shallow, central floor tunnel carrying the torsional strength of the body through the critical cockpit area. Integral with the body was a roll-over hoop.

Suspension and steering was based on 911 philosophy – indeed, the whole of the front suspension including struts, longitudinal torsion bars and rack-and-pinion steering, came intact from the 911. Because of the 914's engine position, transverse torsion bars could not be used at the rear so the semitrailing arms were sprung on coils, a Porsche first. There were, of course, two engine options, the VW 80bhp four and the 911T's six developing 110bhp: the two versions were named the 914/4 and 914/6 respectively. The 914 made its debut at Frankfurt in September 1969.

The 914/4s were assembled *in toto* at Osnabruck, but only the trimmed and painted 914/6

Left: Steel wheels and hubcaps mean this is a 914/4. Bright colors – orange, lime green and yellow as seen here – were all the rage in the mid-1970s.

shells were produced there, the rest of the assembly taking place on the 911 line at Stuttgart. Thus the 914/6s were made to Porsche rather than VW standards.

It is fashionable to knock the 914 as a mistake and part of the reason for this is that it was fairly heavily criticized by the press soon after it appeared. In the United States *Car and Driver* claimed that 'It's about half the cost of a 911S – and about half as good.' The same reviewer lambasted the performance: 'There are never any bright spots in the performance to offset the annoyance.' In reality, the problem with the car was not that it was slow, or handled poorly, but that everyone expected it to revolutionize sports cars in general – they expected it to be sensational, and it was merely very good. The car also received scorn for the rather austere nature of the trim and finish and, of course, for its looks.

The model which really suffered was the 914/6 although initial sales in America looked encouraging. However, there was not much in it pricewise between the 914/6 and the 911, and customers chose the 911. By the end of 1970, barely a year after its announcement, it was becoming obvious that the 914/6 was a non-starter, in spite of reasonably good press reviews this time. But the combination of its looks, its Volks-Porsche nickname (shortened to VoPo, which horrified the VW and Porsche management, since it was also the nickname of the terrifying East German border guards), and a price too close to that of the 911, killed it. The 914/6 lasted less than three model years, with only a handful made in 1972, for a total of 3360. Naturally, when it went out of production, it became an instant cult classic.

The 914/4 soldiered on for some years, however. When the 914/6 was dropped VW intro-

duced a fuel-injected 1971cc engine, which gave the more humble model a performance approaching that of the six. The base version's 1.7-liter engine was also replaced by a slightly larger, 1.8-liter unit. All in all, some 115,596 four-cylinder VW-Porsches were built. This must make it a success: by comparison, only 72,520 Jaguar XKEs were made, and the XKE was one of the most popular sports cars ever.

To drive, the 914/4 feels solid and Teutonic. There is not a creak, rattle or groan out of place (the model I drove was a 1971 1.7-liter version with a genuine 40,000 miles on the speedometer), all systems work well, and it is the sort of car anyone

Below: What might have been . . . unfortunately the 916 was killed off before it appeared in public.

can climb into immediately and feel at ease. On the other hand, it feels slightly desensitized, rather anonymous – it does not have a strong personality.

The gearchange took a while to assimilate. The gate is very narrow, with first out on a limb, left and back. There is quite a lot of 2/3 plane biasing, so going from first to second is almost a straight push forward, but care must be taken going into fourth. In general, the change was very VW, light but with that slight rubberiness at the end of lever travel, and with unbeatable synchromesh.

The steering, compared to something like a Lotus Europa, feels slightly dead, low-geared and ponderous, but, compared to almost anything else, it is light and accurate. Handling and road holding can best be described as purposeful: there is little roll, and even up to highish cornering speeds it simply goes where you point it. Remembering the age of the car I did not push it too hard when I tried it, but it behaved absolutely predictably, neutral and vice free, and I reckon you would have to be doing something very silly to find out that mid-engined cars have a low polar moment of inertia and can spin like a top if you go beyond the limit. It was also a comfortable car, with plenty of room all round and supportive seats. It did not suffer from the traditional drawbacks of mid-engined cars: there is plenty of luggage space in front and back (though none in the cockpit), and there were no major blind spots. Mind you, getting at the engine is not the easiest of jobs.

However, the 914/4 and 914/6 were not the end of the 914 story. Porsche being Porsche, there had to be a competition version. This was called the 914/6GT, and featured a more powerful – though still 2-liter – engine, wide, flared wheel-arches, and competition-tuned suspension. These cars had two notable performances: one finished sixth overall and won the GT category at Le Mans in 1970, and three filled the first three places on the 1970 Marathon de la Route. The 914/6GT gave Porsche ideas: perhaps this was the route to follow, with a bigger engine, and a much more expensive image. Why not make it a direct competitor to Ferrari's Dino? Development work began on the new model in mid-1971, ready for 1972.

It would be given a new name: the 916. Under the wire hatch that served as an engine cover and cooling air intake went the fuel-injected 2.4-liter flat six from the 911S. The track was increased front and rear to take 7-inch alloy wheels shod with 185/70x15 tires. Suspension modifications included antiroll bars front and rear, and ventilated disk brakes.

The most striking feature of the new model was its looks. The distinctive 914/6GT flared arches gave it an astonishingly aggressive appearance. The hideous black rectangular bumpers were replaced by glass-fiber moldings color-keyed to the car which, on the majority of the 916s built, was pure white. The front molding incorporated low-mounted driving lights, an opening for the oil cooler air, and deep, forward-facing spoilers either

Above: Sensational is the only way to describe the 916. With its fat flared arches and tires and all-white color scheme it looked glorious and had a performance to match, thanks to its 2.4 liter 911 engine.

side. The roof was made of steel and fixed in place. The interior was trimmed in white leather, with black used for dashboard and carpeting. It looked mean and, with its all-white color-scheme, very dramatic: the antithesis of the standard car.

Some twenty 916s were prepared for the car's launch at the Paris Motor Show in October 1971. Pamphlets were printed, official pictures taken – and then, two weeks before the opening of the show, the project was cancelled. The 916 would not see production after all. The marketing people were not at all sure they could sell enough to make it profitable. It was a casualty even before it had been seen in public.

The cars themselves went to members of the family and special customers. Some escaped, though, and I have had the luck to drive one. In fact, it was not even a standard 916. It was fitted with even wider wheels, 8 inches at the front and 9 inches at the rear, while the power unit was nothing less than that from a 2.7 Carrera. The 916 weighs 2200 lb, the Carrera 2000 lb, so their performances were comparable. And what a performance! Use all the revs and that magnificent flat six simply propels you into middle distance – you are there before you have caught up with yourself. Below about 3500rpm it just feels quite quick, but then the engine comes on cam, the exhaust and engine note change from that unique beat to an exhilarating, spine-tingling growl, and suddenly you are far beyond the legal speed limits – I saw 120mph with almost contemptuous ease (Porsche figures for the 2.4-liter version were a top speed of 145mph and less than 7 seconds to 60mph from a standstill). Straight-line performance is, in a word, shattering.

The steering is remarkably accurate, ultralight and sensitive. On short trips it is perfect, but on freeways it requires quite a lot of concentration – just a reflex action when changing gears is enough to twitch the car. Driving it around town is, in fact, a revelation. The engine is very flexible and tract-

able, without any flat spots, and the controls nicely weighted, though the pedals are offset toward the center. The gearchange is an enigma: if you are concentrating, third suddenly becomes lost in the (surprisingly, remembering the 914/4) rather wide gate. Forget about it, though, and the gears slur one into the next. Road holding and handling were, like the performance, sensational: my personal fear factor ran out long before the grip from the fat Pirellis. This is about as near as I have ever been to driving a racer on the road. In spite of which, the ride is more than acceptable, firm but not jostly.

The 916, ultrarare, highly desirable, would have been, I feel, a bold and successful addition to the range, remembering how such other 'unsellable' models as the 2.7 Carrera took off. However, the 916 was not the ultimate example of the 914 philosophy. Two cars were built with the racing 3-liter flat-eight engine tucked in the tail. One was given to Ferry Porsche on his sixtieth birthday, the other was used by Ferdinand Piëch. By all accounts, they were staggering machines, but obviously not really suitable for mass production. Still, we mortals can but dream . . .

Above: A number of attempts were made by coachbuilders to reclothe the 914 – this was one by Eurostyle.

Left: From certain angles, and with the right color scheme, the 914 could be quite a stunner, as this 1971 914/6 proves.

THE FRONT-ENGINE REVOLUTION

It seems strange to think of it now, considering how successful the company is (and was back in the 1950s) but in the late 1960s and early 1970s VW was having a rough time. The problem was the Beetle – or, rather, the Beetle's replacement. Neither the type 3, type 4 or the 411 looked as if they would take the world by storm, and certainly not sell in Beetle quantities. One project that looked promising was a design by Ferdinand Piëch, the VW EA266. It was technically fascinating, with its in-line water-cooled four-cylinder engine lying transversely under the rear seat. It might have done for the rear-engined car what the Mini had done for front-engined cars.

However, the resignation of Lotz from the board in 1971 saw a new head at the helm, an engineer called Rudolf Leiding. He was convinced that a complete reversal of policy was required: out went engines in the tail, in came front-wheel-drive, a layout that was sweeping Europe at the time. Exit EA266, and with it the potential for another cheap Porsche, for the Stuttgarters had been working on a sporting derivative as well for their own consumption. Leiding also propounded the 'building block' principle as used by Ford: make the minimum number of engines, bodies and chassis but the maximum number of models and variants by swopping components.

Within the VW group there was one company which had long experience of front-wheel-drive: Audi. Two of the models they had on the stocks, the 50 and 80, could be rebadged as VWs, which they were, and the Passat and Polo were born. At the same time Leiding galvanized his own engineers to come up with a model roughly between both. This they did: it was called the Golf, and the true successor to the Beetle was born in 1974.

Naturally, the cancellation of the EA266 project was a blow to Porsche, not only because it took away the potential for a return to basics with a small, cheap sports car, but also because it left many of the engineers in the research and development department potentially without a job. However, Leiding wanted a sporting car to top off the range, something like the Audi 100 coupé but more sporting again, or the 914. An image leader, if you like. He, therefore, gave Porsche a contract to develop such a car, coded at VW as the EA425.

And then Leiding went. His visions had proved successful but costly. He in turn was replaced by an ex-Ford man, Toni Schmücker. He had to make economies, and besides which the sports-car market did not look too healthy following the Arab oil embargo in 1973 and 1974 (Schmücker took over in late 1974). He in turn cancelled EA425. But by then much of the work had been done and the

Above and above right: The 924 didn't have quite the successful racing career of the 911, but some were raced: this is the AFN 924 which took the British 24-hour record in 1978.

Far right: The 924 has been Porsche's best seller to date – Ferry Porsche poses for the customary photograph with the 100,000th example built.

Previous pages: The same basic body shell serves both the 924 and the 944. The row of air vents across the nose prove this to be a 924 Turbo.

new model was nearing production. Porsche took a gamble. They too reckoned the 911, like the Beetle, could not soldier on forever (just how wrong can you be?) and were looking, again not for the first and last time, for a possible replacement. Why not take over EA425 themselves?

A deal was negotiated whereby Porsche did just that. In addition, there was some mutual back-scratching. One of Schmücker's economies had been to threaten to close down the VW-Audi plant at Neckarsulm, where the brilliant but flawed NSU Ro80 had been made. As an extension to the deal to take over the EA425 as a Porsche, VW-Audi would make it, under Porsche supervision, at Neckarsulm. That way Schmücker did not have to sack the workforce and Porsche would have additional production capacity as well.

The car Porsche had designed for VW-Audi, given Porsche project number 924, took much from the bigger company's parts bin but the bits were juggled around quite considerably. The Audi 100 was a front-wheel-drive car, with the engine arranged longitudinally in the nose and the gearbox immediately behind it. With this package, Porsche had four options: use it complete to form a front-wheel-drive layout: take the whole lot to the back and reverse it, giving a 911-type layout; take it to the back again but keep

it as it was, giving a mid-engined layout; or, somehow, contrive a front-engined, rear-wheel-drive layout. They opted for the latter.

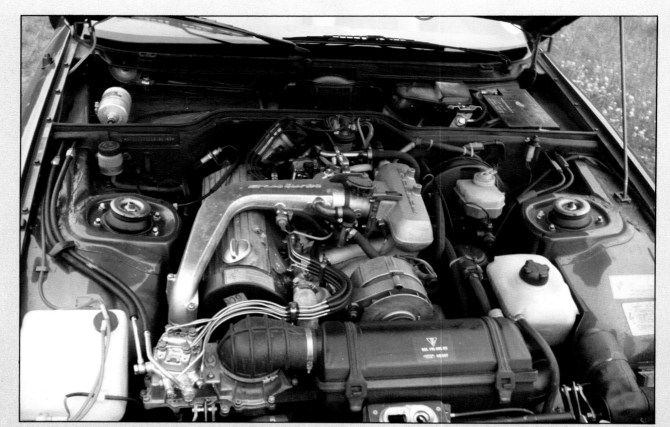

Right: The 924 Turbo's engine bay was well filled! The Bosch fuel-injection system dominates in this view.

Front-wheel-drive was out since, naturally, they envisaged high-power versions, and it would be asking too much of the tires and suspension to cope with both power and steering. A 911-type setup was out too – everyone knew it was obsolete. A mid-engined configuration was good for image and road manners, but was not really practical – and, to attract new customers, the 924 had to be practical. Thus the most practical layout of all, front-engined, rear-wheel-drive, it had to be.

Much was made at the launch of the new model about how the gearbox was put at the back in the interests of weight balance and so on. Agreed, it can help, but the real reason for doing so was that the existing gearbox could be used without any major modifications. In fact, such layouts had been used by others, notably Lancia, before with success. It was a fairly easy job to connect engine and gearbox with a propeller shaft. In this application, Porsche opted for a very slim shaft – less than an inch in diameter – carried in a tube that connected engine and transaxle. Note that this is not a backbone, since it does not carry any body/chassis loads.

The engine itself was the Audi slant four that saw service in the 100 (and in a VW van, and, in of all things, the AMC Gremlin, though, in spite of being German-built, it did not help). It was a single overhead camshaft unit, water-cooled (Porsche traditions dropped like flies with the 924) with a Heron head (the combustion chamber was in the pistons, not in the bottom of the head). In the 924 application it came equipped with Bosch K-Jetronic fuel injection, and gave 125bhp at 5800rpm (or 95bhp at 5600rpm in American, de-toxed, form). Being water-cooled, there were two immediate advantages: the engine was inherently less noisy since the water jackets absorbed some of the noise, and there was a source of heat for the interior. No more fussing about with hot air being blown over the exhaust pipes as in the 911.

Suspension at the front was by MacPherson struts but, unlike those of the 914 which came from the 911, were from the VW-Audi parts bin, the Super Beetle providing the struts themselves and the Golf the wishbones. The Super Beetle also provided the semi-trailing arms at the back, but the springing, via transverse torsion bars, was pure Porsche. Steering was Golf, and braking Audi 100 (disks at the front) and Beetle (drums at the back).

Styling was by Tony Lapine's studio, and, for a VW-Audi, was very Porsche. Audis at the time were of the hard-edged school with, for example,

Below: By using VW mechanicals, the 924 made a return to Porsche traditions. Although designed under contract for the Wolfsburg firm, the lines were near enough Porsche for the Stuttgart company to take it over.

a full-width grille and a boxy roof line. The 924, on the other hand, was almost voluptuously curvaceous, from its rounded nose minus any sort of protuberance (the headlamps popped up) to its high-backed, glass-topped tail. The shape is very difficult to either criticize or praise – it certainly does not have the sleek beauty of the original 911, for example. To me, it is just a little too bulbous, as if somebody attached it to an air line and forgot to say 'when,' but that is only a personal opinion. However, there were two good points: a low (for the time) drag factor of 0.36, and the extensive use of galvanized steel to make the body as rust-proof as possible. Inside there were Porsche front seats, a couple of '+2' devices behind, and a dashboard that was, not surprisingly, more VW-Audi than Porsche.

At the time of its launch, I worked for *Motor* magazine, and not only covered this event but was one of the team that carried out one of the first road tests in the United Kingdom. As with all cars, there were some good features and some bad. The performance was excellent, with a maximum of 125mph as claimed by the factory, and a 0-60mph of 8.2 seconds, and the fuel consumption almost amazing at 25mpg Imp. We liked the clutch and gearchange, found the handling good up to a point ('On faster corners roll oversteer can develop and hence lead to a rather untidy line out of a corner'), the brakes were excellent if a bit light, the interior was very comfortable even if the steering wheel was too low, but we did not care too much for the heating and ventilation or the finish. Believe it or not, the gear-lever knob came off, one of the heater slides stopped working, and it was necessary to be careful when closing the rear window.

However, the worst criticisms were reserved for the ride:

> *On smooth roads . . . it could at times be quite jerky and bouncy, while at low speeds even minor irregularities jarred the body. This is accentuated by poor bump-thump suppression which often makes matters feel worse than they are.*

and refinement:

> *The 924's Achilles heel is that it's too noisy. The engine is raucous, and throbby at high revs which deters spirited driving. Wind noise can also be obtrusive, and road noise – the worst offender of all – is loud.*

This led to an exchange of courtesies between ourselves – me – and Porsche GB, resulting in a member of their staff and myself trying another car. My opinions did not change, and we agreed to differ.

I am still not sure about the 924. Sure, it is a good cross-country car, with a lot of luggage space, relaxing to drive quickly, deceptive in many ways. But, as a confirmed 911 addict, warts and all, I reckon the 924 is and was just a very nice Audi – but even there I have my reservations. The current Audi coupés, quattro or otherwise, are to me simply better cars. Still, many thousands of 924 owners are more than satisfied with their machines, in spite of the criticisms that I and others have made. Perhaps it just goes to prove that we have an over-inflated idea of our own importance . . .

The first modifications to the 924 revolved around the transmission, with an automatic becoming optional in late 1975, and a much-needed five-speed box in 1977, replaced in 1979 by

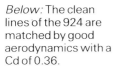

Below: The clean lines of the 924 are matched by good aerodynamics with a Cd of 0.36.

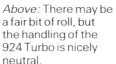

Above: There may be a fair bit of roll, but the handling of the 924 Turbo is nicely neutral.

another Audi-derived box with a more normal five-speed pattern with fifth, not first, as 'the odd one out.' Other changes were gradually phased in: better rubber mountings at the rear plus an anti-roll bar made it quieter and gave even more progression to the already good handling. Trendy black chrome appeared at the same time, as did fully transistorized ignition, and a smaller steering wheel to overcome those complaints about thigh-to-wheel clearance. Just as welcome was the 1982 change that saw better ventilation, and a limited slip differential to help put the power down to the road. And it was at about this time that the original Audi engine was being phased out which would have repercussions in 1985.

The first of the high-performance versions came out in 1979. Porsche chose the obvious route: they added a turbocharger. This was a KKK device, controlled to give 0.7 bar maximum boost via a wastegate, and there was the blow-off valve to keep the turbocharger revs up on the overrun and hence reduce turbo lag. With their vast experience of supercharging, it was a fairly straight-forward installation. Of course, you cannot just bolt on a turbocharger without doing anything to the engine and hope it works: it won't. Thus only the block, crankshaft and connecting rods of the Audi engine were retained intact. Porsche designed a new head with larger, recessed valves on the exhaust side and the spark plugs moved to the induction side. A different combustion-chamber shape allowed a 7.5:1 compression ratio. The result was a pretty useful gain in performance, up from 125bhp to 170bhp at 5500rpm, with torque showing an even more dramatic increase from 122 to 181lb ft at 3500rpm.

There were transmission changes too. A bigger clutch for a start, taking it up to the same diameter as that on the 911. The gearbox was all new and based on that of the 911, since the Audi unit could not cope with all that extra torque. This meant a reversion to the old gearchange pattern, with a dog-leg first. There were fat, 15-inch-diameter alloy wheels, ventilated disk brakes (from the 911 at the front and the 928 at the rear), and a couple of smaller suspension mods.

Externally the 924 Turbo did not look that different. The alloy wheels were one give-away, but more obvious was the plethora of holes that appeared at the front end. There were four across the top of the nose, two more in the air dam for brake cooling, and a NACA duct on the hood. A discreet little polyurethane spoiler around the bottom of the rear glass hatch brought the drag factor down to a very respectable 0.35, the lowest in production at the time.

Supercharging answered at least one criticism of the 924, that it was not powerful enough. Top speed shot up to 140mph (a figure quite easily achievable given any decent uncluttered stretch of road) and the 0-60mph time came down to 7.0 seconds. Porsche did not fit a boost guage, so it was difficult to note exactly when the turbocharger came on song with full throttle, but there was a noticeable surge of power as the tachometer passed the 3000rpm mark. However, it was not sudden, unlike some, and most of the time you could not really tell whether it was working or not: there was just a constant and delicious flow of power all the time, except at very low revs in a high gear. Then, of course, the turbocharger was not giving much if any boost, so the engine felt like what it was, a low-compression 2-liter. Road holding and handling qualities were, as with the standard 924, of a very high order, while refinement had been improved too.

To improve throttle response, and thus flexibility, a year later the turbocharger was replaced with another that was smaller. This meant a slight drop in boost, from 0.7 to 0.6 bar, but by the same token it could react more swiftly to throttle changes, and boost could be felt from as low as 2000rpm. Helping matters along was a Siemens-Hartig digital electronic ignition system which could instantaneously correct the timing and adjust it accordingly, with the result that, apart from

Inset right: The smooth, clean nose of the 928 – the pop-up headlamps were intended to slim the mass of the front down.

Right: One of the limited edition Sebring 924s.

Below: Aggression personified! The 924 Carrera GT in race-ready trim.

improved tractability and flexibility, peak power rose a little to 177bhp, while optional forged alloy wheels plus Pirelli 205/55VR16 P7s gave more bite on the road.

It was the 924 Turbo that formed the basis of what is, to date, the ultimate 924. Like so many before it, this model appeared as a one-off *studie* at Frankfurt in 1979, but to no one's surprise was in limited production by the middle of the next year, as a 400-off homologation special. Because of what it was, it was given a traditional Porsche name: Carrera.

Naturally there was more performance: 210bhp, thanks, among other things, to an intercooler (and, for Le Mans in 1980 this was hauled up to 320bhp at 7000rpm without too much effort). To put this power down, and give racing-type cornering powers, there were dumpy, sticky 215/60VR15 tires on 7J×15 wheels, and to cover these there were wide, flared wheel-arches (looking a bit bolt-on at the back). The front spoiler was deepened and made from polyurethane, as was the slightly bigger rear fender. The NACA duct on the hood was replaced with a raised air scoop, one of the most distinctive parts of the car. Like the 2.7 Carrera before it, the majority of the 400-off cars was sold within weeks of its appearance. For those who wanted to take their racing seriously, there was a GTS version with 245bhp, and its rallying equivalent, the GTR. There was the potential for up to 375bhp with these cars.

However, the 924 derivatives did not set the world's tracks alight as the 911 Carreras had done, and before them the 356 Carreras, and with the introduction of the 944 they were quietly dropped. The days of the 924 looked numbered when the engine was dropped from the Audi range, though VW-Audi kept on building it for Porsche. Since AMC were still using it they did not want to see it vanish, and they took over production of it for a while, but their takeover in turn by Renault soon put a stop to that. Thus the 1986 model year sees what is, in effect, the end of the 924 as we know it, for there is but one model in the range, the 924S – and the significant thing about that is that it is fitted with Porsche's own slant-four engine from the 944. Over 130,000 2-liter 924s were made between 1975 and 1985, which makes it their best seller ever. Perhaps now Porsche's lowest-priced model has lost its Audi image at last?

Potentially the 911's real replacement was unveiled at Frankfurt in 1981. It was called the 944, which indicated a number of things – it was fairly closely related to the 924 which it looked like but it was not just a 924 variant. It slots neatly into the Porsche lineup between the 924 and the 928, 911 country in fact, but is third-generation Porsche in being, like the other two, of the same family with a front-mounted engine and rear-wheel-drive. It is also Porsche's most important current model, their true car of tomorrow, the basis of their future.

The engine in the 944 is pure Porsche. To call it

half of the V8 in the 928 is not really accurate, though it shares some of its dimensions, such as bore and stroke, with the 5-liter eight. Thus it is a slant four of 2.5-liters capacity, which, by today's standards, is a very big capacity for a four-cylinder engine. Big fours, as anyone who has driven behind some of them knows, tend to be rough, to shake a lot. One who realized this as far back as the turn of the century was the British engineer Dr Frederick Lanchester. It was he who suggested that out-of-balance secondary forces could be reduced, or equalled, by adding a couple of weighted shafts running at twice engine speed. This was the principle Porsche adopted: it was a nice touch to see Porsche giving Lanchester the credit for it on the car's launch. With the reputation of the Professor behind them, they could afford to be magnanimous. (Porsche had in fact considered a couple of alternative options, such as a V6 based on the V8, or using the Peugeot-Renault-Volvo (PRV) V6, but settled for the straight four.) The engine gave 163bhp at 5800rpm and 151lb ft torque at 3000rpm.

Engine apart, the major mechanicals came from the 924, while the body was clearly derived from the 924 Carrera. However, the flared wheelarches (which gave the car a much more aggressive look, just as they had done to the 911 years before) were made of steel and blended in more neatly. With this specification, you might be forgiven for thinking that the 944 is a smoother, quick-

er 924. It is, but it is more than that. It is a much nicer car. The extra 38 bhp over the base 924 means that it will zap up to 137mph, passing 60mph from a standstill in 7.2 seconds in the process. More impressive though is its refinement. At idle and low speeds, engine noise is barely a murmur, and all that vibration of the 924 has gone. Accelerate hard and the 944 responds instantly, with turbinelike silkiness. The road holding and handling, on fat Pirelli CN36s, approaches that which a few years ago would have been respectable for an out-and-out racing car, yet, apart from bump-thump which can still be intrusive, the ride is as good as the 924's wasn't. The steering, the controls, the gearchange, all work with a delightful precision. The 944 really is the answer to those who were unimpressed with the 924 as a real

Top: The plush interior of the 924 Turbo is as comfortable as it looks.

Above: Plenty of instruments in the 924 Turbo, but no boost gauge. Porsche deem it unnecessary.

Porsche. It is helped by the fact, of course, that nowadays we accept front engines and rear-wheel-drive as the norm at Porsche, so it should not be judged by 911 standards and handling characteristics.

The 944 was a badly kept secret, with much open speculation about it before it appeared, and none more so than when what was ostensibly a 924GTS ran at Le Mans in June 1981. The bottom half of the engine was pure 944, but there were twin camshafts, four valves per cylinder, and a turbocharger, enough to give the car a top speed of 180mph along the Mulsanne straight since the engine pumped out 410bhp. Obviously with so much potential Porsche would introduce a high-performance version pretty soon, and sure enough at the beginning of 1985 the European press was shuttled out in relays to the South of France to examine and drive the 944 Turbo.

The application of turbocharging to an engine these days is almost a matter of routine to most manufacturers, but not at Porsche. The 944 Turbo's layout is one of the most sophisticated around today, and worth a second look. Working from the inside of the engine outward, forged pistons replace aluminum ones; valve springs have been uprated by about 20 percent; ceramic liners have been cast into the exhaust ports to provide better heat insulation; and the oil-pump output has been increased by 10 percent. But it is the blower installation itself that really repays investigation.

Thus the KKK Type K26 turbocharger is not attached as close to the exhaust ports as possible which is usual practice: instead it is on the inlet side. The reasoning behind this is to keep the thermal loadings to a minimum. In addition, the bearing housing is water-cooled by two circuits, one to control temperatures when the engine is running at full load, the other to prevent a heat buildup when it is switched off, both in the interests of extended turbocharger life. Normally, too, maximum boost is regulated by a fairly simple spring-loaded valve acting as a wastegate to dump excess exhaust gases. Porsche have taken

Opposite: Currently the ultimate 944, the Turbo has a top speed of 150mph.

Below: Engine bay of the 944 Lux complete with 'bunch of bananas' intake manifold.

this a stage further by incorporating a boost pressure-control system into the electronic engine management equipment, which in turn allows the turbine to be supplied with only sufficient gas energy to produce the required boost pressure at the compressor. Claimed advantages of this system include a constant maximum power output, even with energy-sapping exhaust equipment, thus making the 944 the first car to be sold worldwide with the same horsepower rating, 220bhp at 5800rpm, while the torque characteristics can be optimized within the limits of available exhaust gas energy. The addition of a temporary increase in boost pressure can be programmed in for hard acceleration, and antiknock measures can be included by making boost pressure a function of the antiknock controls. A turbocharger is an engineer's dream, a device that gives you something for nothing by using waste materials, but it is also one of those fiendishly simple and cunning devices that require much expertise. The Porsche setup is complicated and expensive, but it sums up absolutely the Porsche way of going about things: identify all the problems, then solve them.

Visually the 944 looks like a mildly customized version of the 924, but in true Porsche fashion nothing is done without a reason and in this case it is all in the interests of better aerodynamics. Gone is the vestigial bumper of the 944: now there is a one-piece polyurethane molding, reinforced with glass fiber, not entirely dissimilar to that of the 928. Apart from acting as a bumper it also incorporates various intakes for the intercooler, radiator, oil cooler and brakes. Working back, the windshield is flush-fitting, there are newly shaped shields for the engine and underfloor areas, glass-fiber reinforced PUR panels beneath the sills between the front and rear wheel-arches, and a special wing beneath the bumper at the back which is not only an instant identity feature but improves underbody aerodynamics as well, all of which give a Cd of 0.33. The interior has come in for attention too, with a new instrument panel incorporating 928-style dials in a 911-shaped pod, electric seat adjustment, and a refined air conditioner.

To drive, the 944 comes perilously close to being boring at times – not because of any flaws but simply because it is so efficient, so good at what it does, that it can seem boring. Undramatic and fuss-free in town, it comes alive on open roads. Speeds, both in a straight line and around corners, rise dramatically but with only a barely perceptible increase in drama. It is as poised and as stable at 120mph as it is at 20mph. On a fairly short straight stretch of autoroute we saw 240kph indicated, near enough 150mph, with almost astonishing ease, which makes Porsche's claim of a maximum of 150mph (and a 0-100kph time of 6.3 seconds) look positively pedestrian.

Apparently, as it later emerged in discussions, the 944 Turbo caused some heated arguments within the ranks of Porsche, since in price and performance its nearest competitor has to be the

911 Carrera. However, chairman of the board, Peter Schutz, who had taken over when Fuhrmann retired in 1981, insisted that it was different enough to sell on its own right without poaching sales from the Carrera. Certainly on the road it is a different animal to the 911, calm, poised, so very efficient, whereas the 911 is excitement, exhilaration, noise, and drama. Both cars excel, but in totally opposite ways.

It is perhaps the latest development in the 944 story that will sell more cars than the Turbo, and which will certainly gladden the hearts of all those who yearn for a convertible Porsche other than the 911, for it is a drop-top 944, shown at Frankfurt in late 1985. A one-off by Bauer, and finished in a rather nasty shade of metallic purple, it is a true convertible, not a Targa, and at the moment is just a *studie*, but then, as we have seen, Porsche *studies* have a habit of going into production.

This brings us to the top of the Porsche range, the 928. In fact, the 928 was conceived just before the 924, but because the latter was using tried components and was backed by VW-Audi, the development time could be drastically shortened:

no such shortcuts could be taken with the 928, which is why it appeared a year and a half later than the 924 at the Geneva Show in 1977.

The thinking behind the 928 was that it should be an upmarket car, more luxurious and more refined than the 911. For years Porsche had avoided Mercedes and Jaguar territory, but they had to admit that there was a market for big, soft, luxury coupés. After all, exhilaration was one thing, but exhilaration between home and office, or home and shop, could become irritation. Jaguar's V12 engine, introduced in 1971, showed that you did not need all the frenzy of the 911's flat six to travel swiftly. The 928 was, therefore, seen as a sort of old man's car, something for the maturer owner, civilized but stylish and more relaxing. Mind you, the market for such sybaritic and selfish machines looked decidedly rocky in the mid-1970s after the Yom Kippur War. It took a steady nerve for Ferry, Fuhrmann and the others to go ahead with a car that was not going to be cheap.

Mounting international legislation on emissions, crash testing, noise suppression, and so on, not to mention the need for a proper heater and a prop-

Above: The Porsche for sybarites. The 928 – this is a 1978 version – is intended for those who put luxury and refinement over sheer performance.

Top: This discreet rear spoiler is one of the few indications that this is the much quicker 928S.

Above: You can't keep Porsches off the tracks – here a 944 leads a 924 in a British club event.

240bhp at 5500rpm and 257lb ft of torque at 3600rpm, rather less than the Turbo's 300bhp and 303lb ft. This would lead to the biggest bone of contention about the 928 it was to suffer.

Power was fed to the gearbox at the back but in this application the box was in front of, not behind, the differential, unlike the 924. There was a choice of five speeds, manually selected, or a three-speed Mercedes-Benz made automatic. Suspension followed racing practice, with twin wishbones and coil springs at the front and lower wishbones with upper transverse links and coils again at the back. However, the whole back suspension was cleverly designed so as to give toe-in when lifting off or braking in a corner, the opposite characteristic most cars adopt, and thus reduced the desire of the car to tuck in at the least, or spin at the worst, under such conditions. This demon back axle was called the Weissach axle, in honor of Porsche's research and development facility. There was power-assisted rack-and-pinion steering, ventilated disk brakes at each corner, and 225/50VR16 Pirelli P7s looked after grip.

The shape was 924 but even more voluptuous and curvaceous. Bumpers were made from a flexible PUR plastic and shaped and color-keyed into the main body so that they were disguised. The result was a rather beaky look to the front when viewing from dead side on, and a rather astonishing rumplike look to the tail. There were pop-up headlamps in the hood but they were not hidden behind covers, remaining visible as on the Lamborghini Miura (according to Tony Lapine, the object here was to reduce the appearance of sheer width, to narrow the hood line, and to give an overall longer look to the car). The styling was controversial: you either loved it or hated it. I was one of the latter . . . Nevertheless, it was distinctly, and distinctively, Porsche.

Porsche awaited the reaction to the car with some trepidation. At first all was euphoria: Ray Hutton of *Autocar* called it: 'The best car in the world,' which must have rankled just a little at Rolls-Royce. The final accolade came when, at the end of 1977, it was voted Car of the Year by a team of international journalists.

But then the grumbling started. With an engine a liter and a half bigger than that in the 911, everyone – especially true Porsche fanatics – expected the 928 to be blindingly quick. It wasn't. In fact, it wasn't even as quick as the 911SC, never mind the 911 Turbo. Yes, it was much more refined but not as refined as some of its competitors such as the Mercedes-Benz 450SLC or the Jaguar XJS. And the Jaguar was quicker on paper (though not on a point-to-point cross-country journey necessarily). Finish, road manners, comfort and build quality were lavishly praised, but refinement and ride were only judged average. They were better than the 911, but only average compared to the opposition: in this respect the engineers at Weissach appeared rather blinkered, judging it merely against the 911.

er automatic, more or less dictated the specification of the 928. Front-mounted engines were better when you threw a car at a concrete block to test its crashworthiness, and better when it came to noise suppression since the twin sources, engine and exhaust, were at separate ends of the car. And there was the question of the hatchback and a bigger boot, too, compared to the 911. So front-engined, rear-wheel-drive it more or less had to be. And, since the 924, being designed and developed concurrently, had its transmission at the back, such a setup was natural for the 928 as well.

Engine choice came down to a V8 since it would give a lower hood line than an in-line or 60 deg V6, and there would not really be room between the wheel-arches for a flat six or eight. Water cooling was chosen for the same reasons as those for the 924: less noise and a source of hot water for the heater. Both block and heads were cast in light alloy, and the cylinders were linerless. Valves were operated by a single overhead camshaft per bank and hydraulic tappets, there was Bosch K-Jetronic fuel injection, and the outputs were

However, the appearance of the 928S in August 1978 seemed to answer all criticisms, for a while at least. On this model a bore increase gave a slightly greater capacity, 4664cc, and upped power to 300bhp at 5900rpm and torque to 282lb ft at 5900rpm, thanks in part to a more sporty cam as well. So that you could tell this was the more sporty variant, not the *Damen*, there was a discreet spoiler around the bottom of the front bumper and around the bottom of the rear window, *à la* 924 Turbo, a little rubbing strake down the side of the doors, and smoother wheels with peripheral slots in place of the normal car's 'telephone-dial' style devices.

This, the pundits said, was much more like it: with a maximum speed of over 150mph, and a 0-60mph time well below 7 seconds, it was close to the Supercar bracket on paper, never mind whether you could actually use such performance or not. So successful was the 928S that in 1982 the standard 4.5-liter car was dropped (as was the 924 Turbo except for the Italian market which has tax incentives for engines of less that 2-liters capacity). Bringing matters up to date, in 1983 the Series 2 version was introduced, with yet more power (310bhp) but better economy and ABS antilock braking as standard. The last round of changes at the time of writing are fairly minor: four piston, light alloy, fixed caliper disk brakes, a quieter exhaust, and minor detailed interior changes. But the press release issued to disclose all these has one line that made me sit up and think: 'The only change to the optional equipment listing is that the standard forged alloy wheels are now available *in platinum* to replace the deleted alternative telephone-dial-style wheels.' I think they mean platinum-colored, but with Porsches you never can tell . . .

To drive, the 928S is like no other Porsche, but then it is like no other Supercar. We on *Autosport* borrowed one to drive to and from Le Mans in 1984, and one of my abiding memories is of a trip taken, just as dawn was breaking, from the circuit to our hotel some 20 miles away. That disarmingly mild woofly American-type V8 sound from the engine takes on a muted but beautifully crisp sound as you use it harder and harder. It felt like a physically heavy car at first, rather like an Aston Martin, but it has a precision and weighting to the steering, and a rocklike steadiness through the corners, which belies its size: like the 911 Turbo, it seems to shrink the more you drive it, and you find you can tuck it into the apex of a corner absolutely accurately, keeping to a neat, very quick line. It has less fuss to it than a 911 Turbo but more than the 944. There was one section of the trip, a series of fast bends, which was taken in one glorious sweep after another, straight-lining the corners wherever possible, that was as exhilarating as in any other car I have driven. I have two final memories of that trip: one when we were stopped by a policeman for no apparent reason. In fact, the gendarme was simply fascinated by the car and its unique registration. It was Porsche GB's demonstrator, numbered THE 928. He just wanted a photograph of it! And the other memory of a privately entered 928 actually taking part in the race. It was, not unnaturally, more than somewhat outclassed in overall terms, but what made it stand out was its determination to finish. Toward the end it seemed to come past each lap on one less cylinder, obviously in dire trouble, but the watching hordes took it to their hearts, cheering it on raucously every time it passed the pits. It made it to the end, finishing 20th. Somehow it seemed to sum up the 928: here was a rather distinguished lady, asked to do something slightly undignified, but doing her best, and doing so very gallantly.

Which is as good a point of any to finish the saga of the road Porsches.

Right: 928 engines under assembly; they are as lovely to look at as they are effective.

Left: Even 928s race occasionally, and this one, an AFN works entry, won the 1983 24 Hour Willhire event at Snetterton.

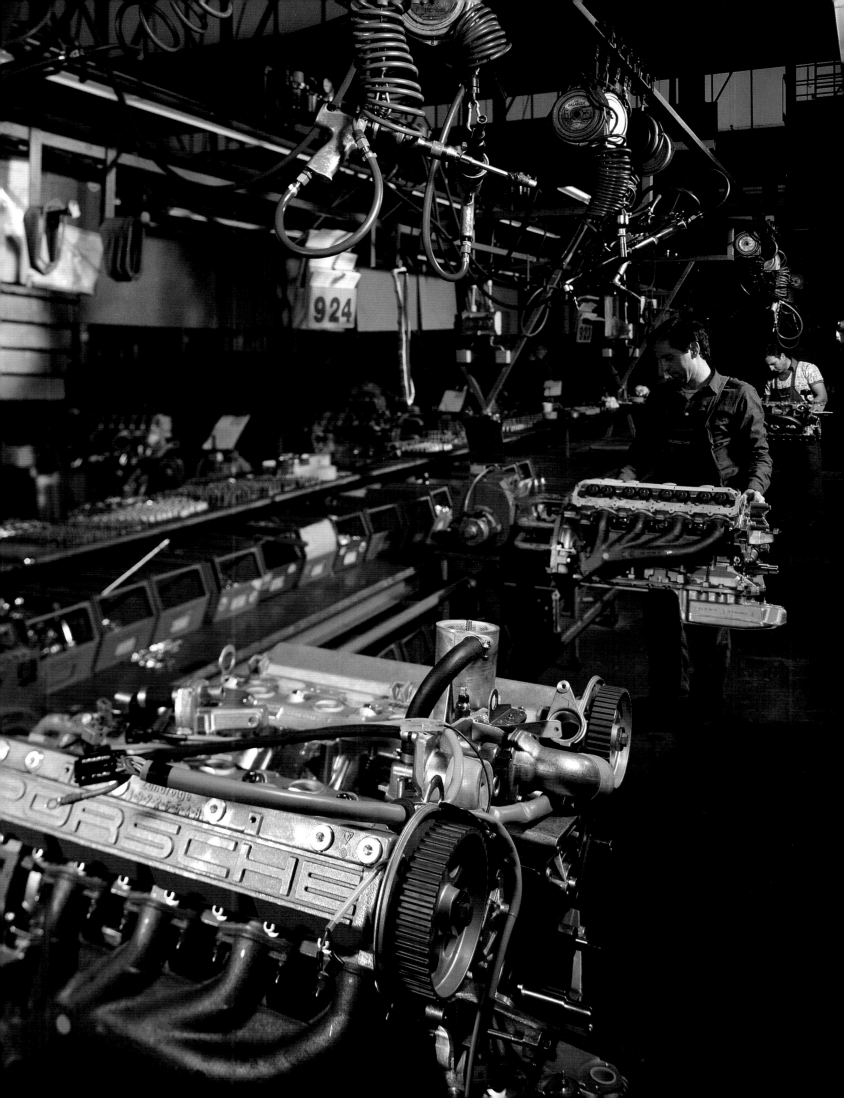

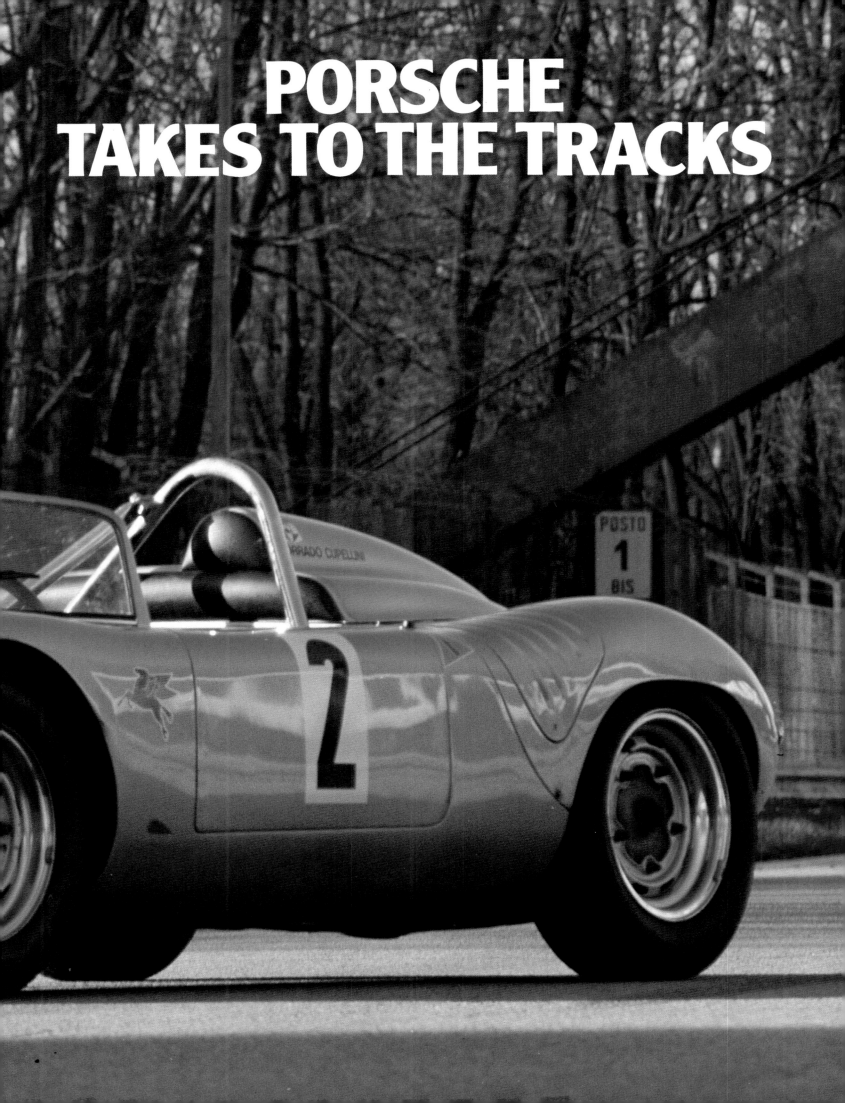

PORSCHE
TAKES TO THE TRACKS

Previous pages: One of the most famous of all racing Porsches was the RSK. This beautifully preserved example, photographed at Monza, is still actively campaigned in historic racing today.

Opposite: Porsche's sports-racing career started with the Type 550 Spyder – this example is an early production car, chassis number 42.

Left: Unlike the 356, the Type 550's engine was between driver and rear wheels, and was the quad-cam Type 547 unit.

Left: The Type 550 was capable of some giant-killing acts on the circuits and was an invariable class winner.

Records show that the first competition success by a Porsche took place on 11 July 1948, with a class win by Professor Ferdinand Porsche's nephew, Herbert Kaes, in a race around the houses of Innsbruck. The car he drove was a little mid-engined open 356 prototype, the very first Porsche. It was a minor victory in a minor race with a car the Porsches considered more a tourer than a racer. It was, though, as the cliché goes, the start of something very big.

Right from the beginning owners took to the tracks, to hillclimbs and rallies, in their Porsches. To own one and not to compete was almost a cardinal sin. In addition, Porsche's policy right from the start of their track career was to offer racers for sale on a commercial basis. Thus, though there have been official works teams and entries, customer participation is of vital importance, and privateers have done as much, if not more, for the Porsche name as the factory has.

Porsche racing cars may not always have been the lightest or the quickest, but they were invariably the best built and, therefore, the most reliable. Nowhere is this more noticeable than at one circuit in particular, where strength and fortitude have to combine with speed: at Le Mans. From 1950 to date there has not been a single year when Porsche has not been represented, and with a fine win by the Jöst Racing Porsche 956B in 1985 – what's more, in the same car that won the year before – the cars from Zuffenhausen have won this classic more times than anyone else, ten to Ferrari's nine. This is not perhaps too surprising when you learn that every new competition Porsche has to survive 1000 km (625 miles) of destructive *pavé* testing at the research and development center at Weissach, something which many production cars would be hard pressed to achieve.

To Porsche, racing is as much a development tool as it is publicity or fun. There is an immense amount of cross-fertilization between the racing and development departments, the two being to all intents and purposes inseparable. This has allowed both racing and road cars to benefit, and given the engineers a breadth of experience unequalled in any other company. Sombody else may have coined the phrase 'racing improves the breed': Porsche proved it.

Strangely enough, though, Porsche seldom innovate, they rarely break new ground. A classic case was the ultimate racing car ever made, the immortal 917. It used a space frame at a time when all the serious opposition had switched to monocoques. Beautifully made, perfectly stressed, superlight it may have been, but it was also simply old-fashioned. The engine, too, only featured two valves per cylinder when four had become *de rigueur* for any self-respecting power unit. The point is, though, that Porsche drew on a vast amount of experience, and the car worked. It won races and that, after all, is the sole function of a racing car.

Right: A 1957 550A. It looks similar to the 550 but under the skin is a totally new space-frame chassis.

Motor racing staggered to its feet fairly slowly in Europe after World War II and new sports cars – when available – were only affordable by the rich, the titled or the well-connected. Thus we find in 1950 Prince Joachim zu Furstenberg and his co-driver, Count Konstantin 'Tin' Berckheim, winning the 1100cc class in the Rally of the Midnight Sun in Sweden, while the ladies award went to Countess Cecelia Koskull in a Gmünd coupé, the first of what could be termed 'serious' wins. Count von der Muhle-Eckart and Rudolf Sauerwein followed this with a second overall and a class win in the Interlaken International Rally. Another result that made enthusiasts stop and think about Porsches came in July 1950, when Otto Mathé took the 1100cc class in the Alpine Rally. Mathé, an Austrian from Innsbruck, had lost his right arm in a pre-war motorcycle accident, and had been one of Porsche's first customers (presumably he had seen Kaes running in the prototype during the Innsbruck races), but one with a difference. His car was fitted with righthand drive so that he could change gear. He had also bought the sole surviving Berlin-Rome Type 60K10 from the family, so must be regarded as one of the very first Porscheophiles.

Late in 1950, the Professor had attended the Paris Motor Show, the first major display in which Porsche had taken part outside the German-speaking countries. While there he met Auguste Veuillet, another Porsche customer who had bought a 1100 coupé in early 1950. He had started a company after World War II called Sonauto to sell uppercrust machines like Delage and Delahaye. Veuillet was offered the Porsche franchise for France and accepted it. Sonauto would become famous for a long time in France as Porsche's distributor.

Above: A rare shot of Von Hanstein at Aintree in 1953 with a Gmünd coupé.

Below: The 550A cockpit.

Veuillet was an enthusiast who had taken part in the first post-war race at Le Mans and he suggested to Porsche that the company should enter the event. The story goes that the Professor asked Veuillet what sort of speeds would be necessary to win the 1100cc class. Veuillet told him, the Professor pulled out his slide rule, worked it all out and agreed it would be possible. At another meeting at the same venue the Professor met an old friend, Charles Faroux, a journalist and one of the people behind Le Mans (and, of course, the intermediary between the Porsche family and the French government which eventually saw the Professor's release from prison). Faroux coaxed the old man to enter the race as well. The Porsches agreed, rather a brave decision since the reaction to the German cars by the French could have been thoroughly nasty.

For this, the first race with a works entry, Porsche relied on the Gmünd coupés. Lighter because of their aluminum bodies, more streamlined because of their smaller roofs, they were modified for the event with extra tankage and much aerodynamic addenda such as spats over all the wheels and fairings under the chassis. However, problems arose. Not with the mechanicals but from accidents. Early in 1951, during a reconnaisance of the circuit, a coupé was written off. Shortly thereafter, the same fate befell another in Germany. The remains of these two cars were cobbled up into one, a spare was prepared, and a two-car team set off for the Sarthe. Then, during the first official night practice, Rudolf Sauerwein crashed at the White House. The team was reduced to one car. This was driven by Veuillet himself and Edmond Mouche. They ran with clockwork regularity. In a car that could reach

Previous pages: Considering how many were made, relatively few Spyders survive – this one, seen in a Porsche parade at the Nürburgring in 1983, is from the Porsche museum.

Despite their low survival rate, Spyders still appear in historic races – Corrado Cupelini's RSK (*far left*) was photographed at Monza prior to the historic event there in 1985, while a similar car (*below*) and an RS60 Spyder (*below left*) are also occasionally seen.

100mph – just – they averaged 73.54mph to finish 20th overall and first in the 750-1100cc class. It was a historic result, possibly more so than any other in Porsche history.

The death of the Professor in January 1951 saw no slackening in the interest in motor racing. That year also saw the climb up the engine-capacity ladder with the introduction of the 1300 and then the Hirth roller-bearing crank 1500. In the Baden-Baden Rally three 1300s were entered, driven by Prince zu Leiningen, Count Berckheim and Richard von Frankenberg. Von Frankenberg's name would be associated strongly with Porsche in years to come, both as a driver and as the editor of the Porsche magazine, *Christophorus*. The Baden-Baden was more race than rally, simply requiring entrants to clock in to as many controls in a given time as possible: the 1300s cleaned up, averaging 75mph for 30 hours – and with a fuel consumption of about 24mpg. You would be hard put to match those figures today.

'Tin' Berckheim won his class in the Travemünde Rally in a 1300, while Messrs Picard and Farge pushed a similar car to a class win and fourth overall in the Tour de France. However, of rather more significance was the long, hard, rough Liège-Rome-Liège Rally. Two Gmünd coupés were entered. One was an 1100 for Peter-max Müller, a special builder of some note (he was German 1100cc-class champion in 1948 and 1949) who had bought a pair of very special heads from Porsche for his VW racer, and his partner Fritz Sittig Huschke Baron von Hanstein. The latter joined Porsche in 1952 to become both racing director and press officer, the Porsche equivalent of Neubauer at Mercedes-Benz with responsibilities on the side for the press. The fact that he

carried out both jobs to the satisfaction of everyone speaks volumes for his ability – and tact. The team of von Hanstein and Müller came home second in class.

The other entry was for a 1500 (officially called a 1300 since the 1500 had yet to be announced in public) and was driven by Paul von Guilleaume and Count von der Mühle. In spite of gearbox trouble, they finished first in the 1500cc class and third overall.

September saw an extended record-breaking session at Monthléry near Paris. An 1100 Gmünd coupé with a 62 bhp alcohol-burning engine ran faultlessly to break 1100cc-class records for 500 miles, 1000km and six hours at 100.3mph, 101.4mph and 101.1mph respectively. An open two-seater special, built by Walter Glöckler, set 1500cc-class figures over the same distances at 116.6mph, 115.3mph and 114.35mph respectively.

The third car was another Gmünd coupé but with one of the new 1500 engines under its rump. This was an experimental unit, giving 72bhp, and was fitted to one of the highly streamlined Le Mans cars even further smoothed out. Porsche prepared the car but the record run was organized and run by Müller and Glöckler, who drove the car along with von Hanstein, von Frankenberg, and Glöckler's engineer Hermann Ramelow. The team was aiming at the 72-hour record in class F, up to 1500cc, and all went well to start with, both 24 and 48 hours being taken easily. A severe setback was suffered when all gears but third disappeared: running as fast as they dared, the drivers eventually completed the full 72 hours at an average speed of 94.66mph. This was not only a class record but a world record. Not a bad debut for the new engine, and it was this car that was

Above: The 1962 Formula 1 car was not a great success. . . .

rushed to Paris for the Show. John Bolster of *Auto-sport* called it a 'splendid publicity stunt,' and Karl Ludvigsen said that it 'went a long way toward legitimizing both the young Porsche marque and the new 1500 engine.'

The 1500's racing debut came in May 1952 in the Mille Miglia. Like the Monthléry car, the Gmünd coupé entered for Counts Berckheim and Lurani (better known as journalist-racer Johnny Lurani) gave 70bhp thanks to a special camshaft designed by Dr Ernst Fuhrmann – the legendary 'Fuhrmann cam' – which allowed the push-rod engines to rev their hearts out. In spite of gearbox trouble again – the VW box just was not proving strong enough for the 1500's torque – they won the 1500GT class against the hordes of homegrown Fiats and OSCAS and such-like opposition.

And so to Le Mans, where once more three of the Gmünd coupés were pressed into service. One was a 1500 and was driven by the French pairing of Lachaize and Martin: it was disqualified in the 19th hour because the driver had not switched off the engine during a refueling stop. One of the 1100s was driven by von Hanstein and Müller but barely lasted six hours before the old bugbear, gearbox problems, sidelined it. The other 1100, however, driven by the previous year's team of Veuillet and Mouche took the 1100cc class once more. It was a good year for Germany: Lang and Riess won overall in a Mercedes-Benz 300SL after Pierre Levegh had blown his Talbot in the last hour while miles in the lead. For the Liège-Rome-Liège event, in which the 1500 had first appeared the year before, Helmut Polensky and Walter

Right: Von Hanstein himself at the wheel of an F1 car during a demonstration run at the Nürburgring in 1983.

Schlüter borrowed a 1500 Gmünd coupé from the quick Belgian lady driver, Gilberte Thirion, and came home first overall, followed by another Porsche in third place driven by a youngster who was having a meteoric rise in the racing firmament, Hans Herrmann. Von Guilleaume was fourth.

By the end of 1952 Porsche's reputation for speed and reliability was already established but so was their reputation for tricky handling. John Gott, a successful rally driver (and a senior police officer in England) wrote one of the first critical analyses of Porsche road behavior, summing it up succinctly when he reported on the 1952 Tulip Rally for *Autosport*:

The Tulip Rally, in which Ray Brookes and I drove my 1947 HRG, gave me a chance to meet the Porsches in direct competition for the first time ... whilst cruising at around 75mph I was startled to be passed by a Porsche which had left Brussels 28 minutes behind me ... I was not unduly shocked when Porsches took eight of the 10 class placings in the timed climb on the Ballon d'Alsace, and von der Mühle's time was only beaten by eight cars in the whole entry, all of these being in the unlimited sports class.

I counted myself extremely lucky to finish fourth at Zandvoort, and certainly would not have done this had not three Porsches displayed a defect in roadholding and crashed into the sand dunes.

Observing these unpleasant sights from the rear, I came to the conclusion that when driven into corners at the extremely high speeds of which these cars were capable, the combination of swing axle, rear-mounted engine and low *general weight caused a breakaway to come without warning and some violence. The more experienced drivers could control this, but it certainly prevented the less skilful from exploiting the full potential of their cars.*

By the end of 1952 Porsches were spreading across the sea to America, thanks to Max Hoffman. As early as October 1951 Hoffman had won his class in the Mt Equinox Vermont, Hillclimb, in a cabriolet. This impressed Briggs Cunningham and he became the owner of another cabriolet, taking a class victory in some races at Palm Beach Shores, Florida, in December. At the end of 1951 Hoffman bought three of the Gmünd coupés in Le Mans trim (they were catalogued by Porsche as the 356SL) complete with spats and 1500cc engines.

At a race at Pebble Beach, California, in April 1952 there were two 356SLs entered and both had braking problems (those spats could not have helped on shorter, tight circuits). One of the owners was John von Neumann. Like Hoffman, von Neumann was of Austrian extraction, with a passion for racing cars. He owned an establishment in north Hollywood, servicing and selling imported cars. On a trip to New York Hoffman suggested he took a Porsche for a drive. Von Neumann was hooked and became the West Coast distributor for Porsche. He was one of the first to make the name famous in America.

Deciding that he did not need the extra weight and drag of a roof for racing in sunny California, von Neumann removed the roof of his Gmünd coupé and fitted a tonneau cover over most of the cockpit. Thus lightened, the fleet little Porsche

Above: For their first appearance at Le Mans in 1953 the Spyders were fitted with streamlined roofs which cooked their drivers. In spite of this they finished first and second in class.

promptly became the terror of the 1½-liter class, campaigning very successfully in 1952-53. This car may or may not have influenced Porsche, but it seems more than coincidence that, at the time von Neumann was racing it, the company at the instigation of Hoffman was making the mysterious America Roadster, the car that, according to Ludvigsen, 'satisfied the American demand for a raceable Porsche.'

By 1952, however, something else was becoming quite clear. There was a new breed of sports car appearing, geared specifically for the circuits, though just driveable on the roads - cars like the C-type Jaguar and the 300SL Mercedes-Benz. More worryingly, they were appearing in the Porsche classes as well – cars like the OSCAs and Gordinis, of minimum weight and stripped of any creature comforts. You could take your grandmother to the shops in a Porsche: such a trip would be difficult in the others. And, while the successes the Porsches did achieve were all the more laudable because of their production background, nobody remembers who finished second. What was needed was a sports racer. Fortunately, there was one who could help out here: Walter Glöckler.

After the World War II Glöckler had obtained a VW dealership in Frankfurt and had prospered mightily. He was also a racing enthusiast who decided to take to the tracks in a special. Obviously, it would be based on a VW, which was where

all the running gear came from. To design the car he enlisted the help of Hermann Ramelow, an ex-Adler designer. Ramelow came up with a neat ladder chassis and aerodynamic body which owed more than a passing nod to the pre-war record breakers of Mercedes-Benz and Auto Union, and to the Mille Miglia BMWs. It was short but smooth, and about the only thing that broke the airflow was the driver's head. The power unit was an 1100 Porsche flat four but this time placed twixt driver and rear axle. Thus the rear suspension was an almost faithful copy of the original prototype of 1948. Beautifully made and ultra-light, Glöckler became 1100cc sports-car champion of Germany in 1950 in the car.

Porsche was naturally pleased with his success and started giving him help in the form of the latest engines. In return he called his cars Porsches, thus adding to the company's prestige. The second Glöckler-Porsche was built in 1951 and it too started winning almost immediately. Like the first it was beautifully made but rather less dumpy, flowing smoothly back from its VW headlamps, and the 1500 Porsche engine was mid-mounted. After a successful racing career in Germany, and that record-breaking attempt at Monthléry, it was sold to Hoffman, who had some minor wins with it but it was a tricky beast to handle and it never really repeated the success it had in Glöckler's hands. The third Glöckler special was the break in

Below: A new name, Carrera, enters the Porsche dictionary. Prior to the 1953 Carrera Panamericana, Karl Kling (in car), Huschke von Hanstein (left) and Hans Herrmann pose with one of the entries. Both works cars retired, but a privateer won the 1½-liter class in another 550.

the line, for it was built on a shortened 356 chassis, and was thus rear-engined: it also featured a detachable top. This car helped Glöckler to yet another German championship, and in turn was passed on to Max Hoffman. Possibly the most famous of the Glöckler specials, though, was the fourth, built for Hans Stanek. Its fame arose mainly because it was widely publicized as a Porsche, being badged as such and appearing on the Porsche stands at both Geneva and Frankfurt in 1953. Like the first two but not the third, this beautiful little car was mid-engined (you begin to wonder whether the designers of the time really did understand what polar moment of inertia was all about, since there is a fundamental difference between rear-engined and mid-engined . . .)

Encouraged by the success of the Glöckler cars, in 1952 Ferry Porsche decided to enter the sports-racing arena. He authorized the design of a car, project number 550, and, to go with it, an engine, project number 547.

The 550's chassis followed the Glöckler designs, being of the ladder type, simple and straightforward. Since it was to be mid-engined, the whole of the power package, including rear suspension, was reversed so that, like the 356 prototype, the torsion bars were right at the back, operated by leading rather than trailing arms. Front suspension was pure Porsche with trailing arms and transverse torsion bars. The bodies of the first two were made by the same firm who

made those of the Glöckler cars – Weidenhausen of Frankfurt – out of light alloy. With their protuberant headlamps but squashed rear end they were not the prettiest cars around, but this would be rectified in the cars that followed. The aim with those first two cars was Le Mans, but in a trial race Helm Glöckler (Walter's cousin) managed to beat off Borgward and EMW (the East German team) opposition in the pouring rain at the Nürburgring on 31 May 1953 to make the Type 550 a first-time winner.

Above: An exhausted Herrmann and Linge relax after their epic drive in the 1954 Mille Miglia when they finished sixth overall. Von Frankenberg (right) smiles happily.

Below: One of the works Spyders at Le Mans in 1955.

The new Type 547 engine was not ready for either the 'Ring or Le Mans, and in both these races the new cars used the 1500 Super power plant which, on pump fuel, gave about 80bhp. For Le Mans, too, they were fitted with sleek, tapered roofs in the interests of top speed, though it is doubtful if these were all that effective, and, as they cut down on vision and raised cockpit heat levels, they were not too popular with the drivers. Making his Le Mans debut was Hans Herrmann, paired with Helm Glöckler, while the other car was driven by the two experienced journalist/racers, Richard von Frankenberg and Paul Frère. Under the expert direction of von Hanstein, the two cars ran consistently and rapidly, seldom more than a lap apart, finishing 15th (von Frankenberg/Frère) and 16th (Hermann/Glöckler) and 1-2 in the 1500cc class. In fact they crossed the line exactly the same distance apart as when they had started, so the French officials decided that the von Frankenberg/Frère car had covered the greatest distance and declared them the class winners.

After assorted races elsewhere in Europe for the rest of the season these two prototypes were sold to the Guatemalan Jaroslav Juhan, who entered them for the wild and wonderful Carrera

Panamericana, a race running the length of Mexico which had more in common with the Paris-Dakar than the Mille Miglia. Juhan himself retired, as did both works cars, but the other, driven by José Herrarte, won the 1500cc class. The name Carrera had entered the Porsche dictionary.

However, before the Carrera, at the Nürburgring in August, a third car appeared. Onlookers

Above: The first 550A ready to run.

Below: It rained at Le Mans in 1958! The Behra/Herrmann 718RSK leads the Barth/Frère car through a puddle.

Above: Inside the racing department Von Hanstein (in glasses) in discussion with the mechanics in front of a 550A under construction.

to life was Ernst Fuhrmann, of camshaft fame, and who would later rise to head the company.

Naturally the 547 was an air-cooled flat four, of 1500cc, but for the first time in a Porsche valve operation was by twin camshafts per bank. With four widely spaced shafts to drive, though, Fuhrmann drew on his experiences with the aborted Cisitalia project. Thinking ahead, too, he wanted the engine to be little or no longer than the pushrod unit, 'just in case' it might see light of day in a production 356 (it did, and the car so equipped became the immortal Carrera). He thus eschewed the usual chain or gear drive and settled on a fiendishly complicated system that incorporated no less than nine shafts and 14 bevel gears. The first shaft was driven by, and ran below, the crankshaft. A bevel gear on the other end of this primary shaft drove two more shafts that splayed out either side, more bevel gears on their ends in turn driving the exhaust camshafts. To make life more complicated, this whole system was set up between the cylinders, rather than at one end. Other features of the engine included twin plugs per cylinder and a novel dual-entry cooling fan that produced much more air flow with only a very marginal increase in power drain than a standard configuration.

observed an exhaust pipe akin in diameter to a drainpipe, and heard a sound such as had never issued from a Porsche before. The car did not race and the engine cover remained firmly in place when it was in public. Another Porsche milestone had been reached, however, for under that tail nestled a very special engine indeed. It was the Type 547. The man Ferry Porsche chose to bring it

The initial power output was 110bhp at 7000rpm, but the 547 was highly amenable to tuning and eventually it gave 180bhp. However, it was very complex. It is said that it took a highly skilled mechanic about 120 hours to assemble one (and an unsympathetic driver a fraction of a second to disassemble it!) and Fuhrmann himself is quoted as saying that it took eight hours, with good luck, to set the timing but if tolerances were not spot on this could extend to 15.

When the 547 was fitted to the 550, the rear suspension was redesigned with the torsion bars in front of the engine, thus relieving the tail from suspension loads and giving less tail-up under braking. Porsche's stylist/aerodynamacist, Erwin Kommenda, adjusted the body lines subtly and the classic 550 shape had arrived.

Thus we come to 1954, and the first event of a 550 with the 547 engine: the Mille Miglia, held on May Day. Hans Herrmann and his mechanic Herbert Linge finished a glorious sixth overall and

first in class after an eventful race. Apart from losing some 20 minutes through damp ignition, they rounded one corner at high speed to find a railway barrier slowly descending in front of their eyes. Hermann kept his foot on the throttle, both ducked, and the car shot under the barrier and across the track. The 550 was low . . .

For Le Mans, four cars were entered, all with the 547 engine, though one had a smaller capacity of 1100cc. However, for once the now-legendary Porsche reliability was absent, and incorrect ignition setting (plus, no doubt, the usual French witches' brew that passes for fuel) caused a spate of holed pistons. In the 1500cc class only one car survived, running on three cylinders for a considerable time, but when the class leaders and main opposition in the form of the OSCAs put themselves out through some severe problems in the last few hours, it grumbled across the line in 12th position, the sole survivor and thus winner of its class. The 1100, driven by Paul Stasse and Zora

will, they sold like hot cakes, from two in 1954 to 63 in 1955 and 13 in 1956. One customer Porsche would like to forget was James Dean. He had been a little successful in a Speedster and was killed in his Spyder on the way to a meeting. Porsche also sold some of the ex-works cars. One went to von Neumann for himself and a superbly talented ex-patriate Englishman, Ken Miles, to drive. Ken would give Porsche some splendid wins in 550s between 1954 and 1956.

Porsche soldiered on in 1955 with the 550. For the tragic 1955 Le Mans race they organized matters better and romped home to a 1-2 in both the 1500cc class and the 1100cc class, the highest overall placing being Polensky's and von Frankenberg's fourth (they also took the prestigious Index of Performance, usually a French preserve). In that year the 550 took class wins in the Buenos Aires 1000 kms, the Sebring 12 Hours, the Mille Miglia, and the Tourist Trophy.

However, the 550 had its drawbacks. It was at its best on fast circuits or in long-distance races where its speed and reliability were paramount: on tighter, twistier roads the lighter, more nimble Lotuses and Coopers could see them off. In addition, the suspension was still basically that of the 356. In the right – that is experienced – hands they could be made to corner as quickly as the best of them, but it was hard work and there was a very fine dividing line between just under and just over the limit. John Bolster tried a couple at Monthléry and recalled that one was fine in the corners but highly unstable in a straight line, while the other displayed diametrically opposite characteristics.

Thus 1956 saw a new 550, the 550A (also called confusingly the 1500RS). The main change was a totally new chassis, a space frame replacing the ladder. This not only cut weight but gave three times the torsional stiffness and no less than five times the beam stiffness. Allied to this frame was a revised rear suspension which used a low pivot arrangement *à la* Mercedes-Benz, thus removing much of the 'clap hands' characteristics of the basic swing axle. Engine power had risen to between 130 and 135bhp, and there was a five-speed gearbox, really a four-speeder with an additional first for starting, sharing space with reverse inside the gearbox casing.

The first outing for a 550A in 1956 was in the Mille Miglia, where it retired, but a bare month later two young lions, Wolfgang von Trips and Umberto Maglioli, brought one home to a fourth overall at the Nürburgring 1000 kms. Another Porsche entrant for this event was a young Swiss, Michael May. His car, somewhat battered around the edges, sported a huge wing placed centrally over the cockpit which could be feathered on the straights but angled downward in the corners. He astonished everyone but himself by lapping faster than the works cars in practice, but the spoil-sport organizers, aided and abetted by Porsche, promptly banned the device.

Then, in June 1956, the 550A gave Porsche one

Arkus-Duntov, the 'Father of the Corvette' as he later became known, came home 14th, also the only class survivor.

For the rest of the year the 550s were usually unbeatable in their class, though a relative newcomer, a company called Lotus, gave them food for thought at Silverstone. They were giving bigger-engined machines a run for their money. One such dramatic portent came in the 1954 Carrera Panamericana, the last to be run, when Herrmann finished a magnificent fighting third, with Juhan behind him in fourth in another 550. Naturally they won their class by a country mile.

Late in 1954 customer 550s started to appear, with bodies by a new supplier, Wendler. The official designation was 550/1500RS: 550 for the project type number, 1500 for the capacity, and RS for *rennsport*, or racing sport. However, just to complicate matters, Hoffman reckoned this was far too many numbers and letters, so he suggested the cars be called Spyders. Call them what you of their most sensational wins in a race that would give its name to a Porsche line: the Targa Florio. The entry was almost an afterthought. Only one car was sent, hastily painted white by Huscke von Hanstein and its driver, Umberto Maglioli, and only two mechanics tended it. In spite of competition which included Castellotti in a Monza Ferrari and Taruffi in a 300S Maserati, Maglioli drove tenaciously and, nearly eight hours after the start, climbed stiffly from the cockpit, having driven single-handed. If the result was not Porsche's first giant killing act, it was the first major outright win of massive significance.

After that splendid effort, Le Mans was almost a let down. Porsche entered two 550As, both coupés with roofs which lifted as an entity with the tail to give engine access, looking similar to those which had run in 1953. In truly awful conditions (which must have made the drivers pleased with their closed cars) one works car retired, as did both of the supporting customer 550s, but the von Frankenberg/von Trips car droned round to a fifth overall and also took the by now inevitable first in class.

One race, won by 'Taffy' von Trips in a 550A, took place at the Avus, a Berlin circuit consisting of two parallel straights joined at each end by high, steep bankings. One of the official works entries was a very special 550A, nicknamed Mickey Mouse (a reference to its handling) by von Frankenberg. It was, in effect, a shorter, slimmer, lighter more streamlined 550A, with a magnesium body, a pointy nose, and a much flatter shape. It finished fourth at the Solitude circuit in July driven by von Frankenberg, but its main claim to fame came at that Avus meeting. While in the lead – proving that there was nothing wrong with the shape as far as sheer top speed was concerned – von Frankenberg exited stage left, disappearing over the top

of the banking in one of the most frightening accidents ever recorded. He miraculously survived, relatively unscathed.

Development work on the 550A carried on during the 1956/57 winter, drawing on the lessons from Mickey Mouse, that lightness and a smaller frontal area could be beneficial. The headlamps were placed behind plastic fairings, and a much slimmer, lower, lighter car was created. One major revision was a redesign to the front suspension. The upper tubes which carried the torsion bars were angled down toward the center of the bottom tube: looked at from the front the system resembled the letter K lying on its side. The car was dubbed the RSK, although it had a Porsche Type number, the 718, which became a generic identification to cover not just the succeeding RSKs but the F1 and F2 racers as well. In fact, the K configuration front suspension did not last very long but the name stuck.

The only major race for the RSK in 1957 was at Le Mans, heading the regular 550As. For this race it was fitted with a wrap-around windshield and square tail fins, the latter an attempt to improve straight-line stability. It was very quick but was eliminated in a crash with Tony Brooks' Aston Martin. Driving it was Maglioli and Edgar Barth, an East German who had driven for the EMW team. Following his successes in the West German Porsches, he was declared *persona non grata* in his homeland so settled in the West to become one of Porsche's best drivers. In the race itself both the other works 550As retired (the Storez/Crawford car ran out of fuel with less than an hour to go) and it was left to the American-entered white and blue 550A of Hugus and de Beaufort to take the traditional 1500cc class. Not for the first or last time a private entry upheld Porsche honors.

The 550A formed the backbone of the works team in 1957, but toward the end of the year Porsche produced enlarged versions of the 547 engine, with capacities of 1587cc and 1697cc, so that they could enter the 1600 and 2-liter classes in the European Hillclimb Championship and which could bring the RSKs into another category in 1958. Since the RSK was to head the team in 1958 extensive work was carried out on it during the winter of 1957. This led to the reversion to a straight tube for the front suspension, not the K from the name, while there was a major change to the rear suspension: gone were torsion bars, replaced by coil springs and a Watts linkage.

The RSKs were not ready for the first race of the year in Buenos Aires, but that was not important since Porsche's latest recruit, the Grand Prix driver Jean Behra, and Stirling Moss, having a one-off drive, came home third, only 8 seconds behind the winner, in a 550A with a 1600cc engine. A sign of the times, and one which gave Porsche food for thought, was that a week before this event Moss had won the Argentine Grand Prix in his little, underpowered, no-hoper Cooper.

Behra, the volatile, one-eared little Frenchman, gave Porsche a second overall in the Targa. He followed this up by giving the 3-liter machines such as the Ferraris and Astons a run for their money at Le Mans and, with co-driver Herrmann, finished third and topped the 2-liter class in a 1.6-liter car. In fourth place came Barth and Frère in a 1500, naturally taking their class as well. The Behra/Herrmann car was not fitted with fins on the tail, the Barth/Frère car was: some drivers swore by them, others hated them. Either way their overall effect, perceived or not, seemed marginal – they were not used at the Avus, for example, the one circuit where they should have worked well. Another significant result came at the Los Angeles Times Grand Prix in October 1958, with Behra again placing fourth against strong, and much more powerful, opposition, in what Karl Ludvigsen called the 'First major professional sports-car contest in post-war America.'

Von Frankenberg's amazing accident in 'Mickey Mouse,' the ultraslim RSK, at the Avus. *Left:* The start of it, as the car hops over the edge, and (*right*) looping the loop. Von Frankenberg emerged relatively unscathed.

Left: For Le Mans 1956 the Spyders once more appeared with coupé roofs. This is the class-winning Von Frankenberg/Von Trips car hammering through White House.

The car which Behra used to good effect in Los Angeles had a glorious career, giving Joe Buzetta the SCCA Class F Championship as late as 1962. The RSK became exceedingly popular with customers, just as the 550 and 550A had been, and private successes with it in the late 1950s and early 1960s were innumerable. For 1959 the works again relied on the RSKs, refined and more powerful, but they had other things on their plate, such as the F2 and F1 program, and Le Mans was a debacle: six Porsches started, none finished. It was Porsche's worst year ever. The only consolation was that Barth and Seidel had cleaned up the Targa Florio.

The major change for this season was the adoption of, at last, twin wishbone rear suspension for the first time on a Porsche. Of the two cars entered for the Targa, in fact, one was a 1.6 with the new setup but it retired, the Barth/Seidel car being a 1.5 standard RSK.

The Avus event in August saw not one but two repeats of the famous von Frankenberg incident. The Dutchman, Count Carel Godin de Beaufort, nearly caused a riot among officials when; having gone over the banking in his privately entered car, he found himself in the paddock and, with considerable aplomb, promptly motored back into the race. More tragically, Behra in one of the works cars skidded in the damp conditions and his car hit a concrete bollard at the top of the banking. The popular, press-on-regardless, brave little Frenchman lost his life instantly.

For 1960 there were some new international regulations which called for wider cockpits, bigger windshields, room for a suitcase and a spare wheel. Porsche adapted the RSK to these new regulations, adding 4 inches to the wheelbase in the interests of better handling too, and called the new versions RS60s.

Like the RSKs and 550s before them, the RS60s carried on winning, and by now too Porsche were hiring more and more Grand Prix drivers like Graham Hill and Jo Bonnier, but it was the taciturn Belgian Olivier Gendebien and Hans Herrmann who won overall at Sebring, while Bonnier and Herrmann again pulled off the hat-trick at the Targa, a race that was rapidly becoming Porsche's own. A mixture of the previous teams, Bonnier and Gendebien, won at the Nürburgring. Le Mans, however, was another story, and almost a repeat of the year before. The highest-placed works car was the Barth/Seidel RS60 in 11th place, with only two gears left. Trintignant and Herrmann retired early with a broken con rod, and the fastest car, driven by Bonnier and Hill, cracked a piston. Linge and Walter retained some Porsche credibility by finishing sixth overall and first in class in a works Carrera.

With the factory preoccupied with single-seater racing in 1961, the RS60 became the RS61 with barely a single change. In spite of that the customers loved them, and Bob Holbert used RS61s to win the SCCA E Sports

Racing class in 1961 and 1962. For themselves, Porsche developed a trio of specials on the 718 base. Two were coupés, styled by Butzi Porsche, with big windshield and tops that were abruptly chopped off at the back. The third was an open Spyder, called the W-RS. This had a wheelbase 4 inches longer than the standard 718.

For the Targa, there were three cars entered, the W-RS and two RS61s, one a semiworks entry for Moss and Hill by the American Camoradi team, who led until a couple of miles from the finish when the differential gave up. The W-RS, driven by Gurney and Bonnier, finished second – behind a rear-engined Ferrari. At Le Mans all three 718 specials were entered, powered by plain-bearing versions of the 547 engine. The W-RS, driven by the American pairing of Masten Gregory and Bob Holbert, took fifth overall and the 2-liter class, with Barth and Herrmann trailing them in one of the coupés. From then on these three cars were rebuilt with the eight-cylinder sports-racing version of the Grand Prix engine, and this effectively saw the end of the Type 547 and its derivatives in top-drawer works-backed entries.

Above: A slightly battered Spyder? Not surprising, really – this is de Beaufort calmly motoring back into the race after *his* spectacular 'over the top' incident at the Avus.

Left: Only the regulation height windshield spoils the lines of the supersmooth RS60. Note regulation soft top folded behind the seats!

Thus 1962 saw a 718 coupé and the W-RS entered for the Sicilian classic, the Targa Florio, by Count Florio's Scuderia SSS Republica de Venezia. The W-RS, finished in the usual Porsche silver, crashed, but the coupé, painted in the most curious shade of flat red, struggled on, minus brakes, to finish third. And they were back again in 1963 (Porsche entered the GT category at Le Mans in 1962 with Abarth Carreras) in the same race, though this time featuring a fundamental change to the suspension with the adoption of F1-type wishbones at the front, some panels made from glass fiber, and tweaked engines. It was the coupé's turn, driven by Bonnier and Carlo Abate, to win at record speed. The same two cars reappeared at Le Mans in 1963, and the W-RS was the only one to reach the end, in eighth place, after an eventful race in which a rear wheel fell off and Barth pushed it to the pits.

The W-RS had a very strenuous life and became one of the best-known and loved Porsches. It was sent to America for a while and on its return was used by Edgar Barth in the European Hillclimb Championship, which he won two years in a row, in 1963 and 1964. In 1964 it turned up in Sicily for the third time, in the Targa, with Hill and Bonnier at the helm, but retired with half-shaft trouble. This old faithful car was affectionately nicknamed *Grossmutter*, or grandmother, and when Edgar Barth died in 1964 it too was retired.

However, in the late 1950s Porsche did not just concentrate on sports racers. There were two other categories in which they took a more than passing interest: GTs and single seaters.

The competition GTs were, of course, the Carreras, the mixed marriage between the 356 and the Type 547, which is a bit like putting a 963 engine into a 924. Announced in 1955, the original intention was a short run, maybe 50, to keep the GT and rally buffs happy but, like the 2.7 Carrera to come, it became the 356 to be seen in. Pretty soon, however, there were two versions, the Deluxe for those who wanted to pose, and the GT for those who were serious.

In fact, the combination had been seen as early as August 1954, when a Gmünd coupé with a Type 547 aboard, detuned to give about 100bhp, driven by Messrs Polensky and Linge, swept to victory in that most arduous of events, the Liège-Rome-Liège.

The production GT was very spartan, and came in coupé or Speedster guises, the latter being the most coveted. With 110bhp on tap, and its light weight, such a car could and often did see off ostensibly quicker pure sports racers. They made such events as the Liège, the Tour de France, the Mille Miglia and the Alpine theirs – in the sub-2-liter class if not overall. The original 1500s became 1600s with plain bearings, and still won.

The ultimate Carrera was the Abarth Carrera. In an attempt to get a lighter and more compact GT within the rules (which allowed a different body), in 1959 Porsche asked Zagato to build 20 lightweight bodies for the Carrera. To avoid any possible repercussions *vis-à-vis* Zagato and any of his Italian customers, Porsche's old friend Abarth was brought in to act as middle man – since he was well-known for making small rear-engined cars with Zagato bodies, it was assumed that he had simply expanded his line upward. The shape was styled by Franco Scaglione. With its aluminum body and much less frontal area, the Abarth Carrera was a very quick machine. It was an Abarth, driven by Linge and Walter, which saved Porsche at Le Mans in 1960 by taking their class and coming home 11th overall. In fact, Le Mans was a pleasant stamping ground for Abarths – in 1961 Linge and Pon finished 10th and head of class, and in 1962 three formed the official Porsche works team. Barth and Herrmann had a fairly uneventful run apart from some gearbox trouble – and some opposition from a Lotus Elite – to finish seventh overall and first in class, while another, entered by Porsche's old friend Veuillet, and driven by Buchet and Schiller, staggered home, brakeless, in 12th place.

The final 356 GT, though, was the 2000GS/GT, which only saw one season's life, and only two were built before they were replaced by the 904. Looking astonishingly like the 718 coupés of 1961, they too had tunnel tops, but both retired at Le Mans and were, in effect, museum pieces in their own lifetime.

Above: Spiritual ancestor of the single-seater Porsches was Otto Mathé's little ice-racer.

Below: Chassis of the first Formula 1 car, with wishbone front suspension.

Porsche's efforts in single-seater racing came and went, if not ignominiously, then without adding much to their stature, between 1957 and 1962. At the start of that period, a new Formula 2 was announced, which called for engines of not more than 1.5 liters in capacity running on pump fuel. Porsches fell into this category and to start with they entered one or two races experimentally with converted sports cars. The first was to have been at Rheims, using the ex-Le Mans RSK, but it had been too badly damaged to run, so honors were upheld by a customer, Goethals, in a 550A. However, the F2 race at the Nürburgring on 4 August 1957, saw two 550As officially entered. On the rough Eifel circuit Barth won from Roy Salvadori in the lighter, more nimble, but less powerful Cooper single seater.

The next appearance in a single-seater race was at Rheims two weeks after Le Mans in 1958, a fast circuit where the Porsche's better streamlining should prove superior. The Frère/Barth Le Mans car was converted to a central driving position (easy with the Porsche's chassis design and centrally placed steering box), together with a tonneau cover which barely left room for the driver's head, and rear-wheel spats. Behra proved that the lower drag of an all-enveloping body did indeed work by winning the event. The same car came home second to Bruce McLaren in a Cooper at the Nürburgring in August – and sixth overall against full Grand Prix machinery.

It was the announcement in late 1958 that, as from the 1961 season, Formula 1 would be run to a 1.5-liter formula that really made Porsche stop and think. Full-width bodywork would be banned and there would be a 1100-lb minimum weight limit, but these were minor quibbles as far as the Stuttgarters were concerned. Think of it: a single-seater RSK would be, in effect, a full-blown, ready-born Grand Prix car. Ferry gave the go-ahead for an F2, and later an F1, project. Since the basis was the sports car it was given the project number 718/2.

From the RSK came the engine, brakes, track and wheelbase. There was still trailing arm/torsion bar front suspension, but wishbones appeared at the back. The chassis was basically a slimmed-down RSK. Clothing it was a dumpy, typically Porsche-style, body. The engine, of course, was the Type 547 Carrera unit, giving in this application some 150bhp.

In its first appearance at the 1959 Monaco Grand Prix the 718/2 distinguished itself when von Trips, having trouble finding the correct gear out of the possible six available in a gateless box, managed not only to crash himself but took out the only other F2 cars in the field, a Ferrari and a Lotus. In the same event, another single-seater Porsche ran in practice, driven by the young Italian girl Maria-Teresa de Fillipis, but she did not qualify. It had been built for Jean Behra in Italy to a design by Valerio Colotti, and was only raced

Above: Upholder of Porsche honors in the early 1960s in the GT category was the lovely Zagato-bodied Abarth: here the Barth/Linge car leads the class-winning Holbert/Wester Carrera at Sebring.

a few times, its best being a second placing, Herrmann driving, at Rheims behind Moss in a Cooper-Borgward. It is now owned by Murray Smith of New York.

Behind Herrmann in the Behra car at Rheims was the works 718/2 with Jo Bonnier behind the wheel, and the same driver took it to a third and fourth in heats for the Kentish Trophy at Brands Hatch in August that year. The significance of this minor event only became apparent when, a week later, Stirling Moss drove it in tests at Goodwood. The upshot was that Moss's patron, Rob Walker, was offered a car for Moss to drive on a semiworks basis in 1960, which Moss and Walker accepted.

The 1960 season was fairly successful, Moss and the works drivers sharing many wins between them. At Aintree, home of the British contingent, Moss led Bonnier and Graham Hill home to a 1-2-3 victory. For the Solitude Grand Prix in July there were five 718/2s entered, of which one had a much slimmer, neater, albeit not much more elegant body designed by Butzi Porsche. John Surtees retired one, but the others finished in line astern – but, alas, behind the new and nimble rear-engined F2 Ferrari. However, this result was avenged at the last race of the F2 season at Modena, Ferrari's homeground, when Bonnier trumped the Ferraris. The season came to a close with a couple of wins by Moss in South Africa, with Porsche the official (albeit disputed) winner of the 1960 Formula 2 Constructor's Championship.

In 1960 Ferry gave the go-ahead to yet another project, this time an eight-cylinder engine, which in 1½-liter form could be used in F1 and in 2-liter

form in sports cars. The valve train was similar to that of the 547 except that there were two half-speed shafts, one above and one below the crankshaft, to drive the inlet and exhaust camshafts respectively. However, the new Type 753 unit would not be ready in time for the first season of the new 1.5-liter formula, so the 718/2 soldiered on at the start of the year. However, there was a new chassis, slimmer yet again, and at the front twin wishbone suspension at last – the final VW link had been broken. The fuel tanks were relocated for better balance, and the type 547 engine was kitted out with Kugelfischer fuel injection which did not give any more power but made the unit less peaky.

It did not take long to discover that the new cars were pretty hopeless, and after the Dutch Grand Prix at Zandvoort the decision was taken to revert to the old 1960 cars. They were at least a known quantity, and, if they could not keep up with the fleeter lightweights from Britain, they were reliable. Thus Gurney could score a fairly impressive string of seconds, at Rheims, Watkins Glen and Spa.

It is traditional to call Porsche's 1962 Formula 1 season disastrous, but consider the facts. Out of seven World Championship events entered, the score was one first, and a third, fifth, sixth, seventh and ninth, plus a first and a third from two non-championship races. However, it must be said that there was a considerable amount of internal filibustering and politicking going on within the company, not helped when Rabe retired as technical director in 1960 and his successor, von Rück-

Right: World Champion Graham Hill displays some contact with other vehicles in an Abarth-Carrera at Goodwood.

er, himself departed in late 1961 to go to BMW, being replaced by an outsider, Hans Tomola.

For the season there was a new chassis, the Type 804, with a tubular space frame, following then-current practice, wishbone suspension at either end (but with longitudinal torsion bars operated by the top wishbones, which helped make rapid changes of the spring rates possible). Then there was the new flat-eight Type 753 engine, and an even slimmer, lighter body similar to that which Butzi had produced for the 718/2, which cut down on frontal area.

What perhaps really showed that the Type 804, beautifully made though it was, was outdated was a car that appeared at its first race, the Dutch Grand Prix. There on the grid was a super-sleek green and yellow bulletlike projectile which had instantly made the Porsche (and the others, to be honest) obsolete. It was Colin Chapman's monocoque Lotus 25.

The high spot of the season was Gurney's win at the ultrafast Rheims circuit – this was won only when most of the better opposition dropped out, but it was won. Another win in the non-championship race at the Solitude raised morale a little, but that was only a teaser. The Type 804 was not competitive. Before the end of the year Ferry Porsche pulled out of Grand Prix racing. It would not be until 1984 that the sounds of a Porsche engine would be heard in a Grand Prix again – and then it would be for a customer. But what a sound that would be . . .

Below: The elegantly beautiful lines of the Abarth-Carrera still look good in the 1980s.

THE TAKEOVER BID

The beginning of the 1960s had seen Porsche strongly established in the motor-racing firmament. The little 550s and 718s had been, for a decade, well in control of the sub-2-liter sports-car classes, harried occasionally by the lighter, fleeter, but more fragile Lotuses, Coopers and Maseratis. They were looked on rather affectionately as the 'little boys' who might get lucky when the 'big boys' – Ferrari, Maserati or Aston Martin, for example – fell by the wayside, and thus gain an overall win or two. At the beginning of the 1970s, as a total contrast, Porsche were the big boys, and the car to beat on the track was that fearsome, fabulous machine, the 917. Developing some 1100bhp in its final form, it is to date the most powerful racing car ever made.

The late 1950s and early 1960s had been turbulent times for Porsche. The single-seater campaign had not only exhausted hard-earned cash but had proved to be a diversion in the wrong direction. Porsche owners had always been able to identify with the racers but F1 was stretching the link to its limits. Cash and manpower was being funnelled into the 356's successor as well, the 911. It seemed natural to combine the two, to build a new competitive GT car which customers could buy and which Porsche themselves could campaign. The result was the first of a new generation of models, built to a new design philosophy, in which the third generation of the Porsche family, in the shape of Butzi Porsche and Ferdinand Piëch, would prove their mettle. Given project number 904, it was also called the Carrera GTS. Ferry gave the go-ahead for the project late in 1963.

From the start it was intended to take the new flat-six engine from the 911, but this would be mid-mounted and the 904 would, therefore, follow racing, not road, practice. To homologate it for the 2-liter GT Championship at least 1000 would have to be made. However, the flat six was far from ready so the Type 547 twin-cam flat four was installed in its place, although it was attached to the 911's gearbox.

Hans Tomala was head of engineering at Porsche by this time, and under his direction the design of the 904 took place fairly rapidly. The chassis represented something of a break from either the 911 or the 718, for it was of ladder construction. There were deep, rectangular longerons extending from front to rear suspension, which was by wishbones and coil springs all round. Steering

Previous pages: With the arrival of the 90-series cars, Porsche started the climb up the ladder to domination of the sports-racing world: the lovely 908 Spyder shown here was but one of the rungs.

Below: The 904 continued Porsche's winning ways – this is the Davis/Pucci 904 taking the Targa Florio in 1964.

force had to run in the 3-liter prototype class. One of them, driven (and subsequently acquired) by Briggs Cunningham and Lake Underwood, took the class and finished ninth overall. However, the 904's combination of strength and speed was obvious when, almost exactly a month later, a 904 unexpectedly gave Porsche their fifth win in the classic Targa Florio, driven by the local enthusiast Antonio Pucci and Colin Davis, son of the British journalist who had been successful at Le Mans with Bentleys in the 1920s and 1930s. What's more, another 904 followed them home, crewed by Linge and Balzarini.

Naturally the 904 was successful, featuring on the scoreboards in 1964 at such diverse circuits as Spa, Rheims and the Nürburgring, not to mention the semirace, semirally Tour de France. On the whole, Porsche left it to customers to compete in the 904s to such effect that at Le Mans, after the two works 904s retired, privateers finished seventh, eighth, 10th 11th and 12th - and 904s constituted the only type at the Sarthe that year. The company themselves looked to the 904 to give them a successor to the 718 by modifying a clutch of 914s to take the 2-liter eight-cylinder Type 771 engine which had been seen in the W-RS. Two such cars were entered for Le Mans and retired – but not before being clocked at 175mph along the Mulsanne straight. The 904/8s made a couple of other appearances in 1964, a third overall in the Paris 1000 kms at Monthléry being their best placing. Another variant of the 904 retired out of the same race but is worth noting because it had the engine which it was intended should be standard in the 904 all along: the flat six from the 911. As installed in the 904/6 this unit had twin plugs per cylinder and, of course, was still a 2-liter. Adding up all the results, the 904 had won the 2-liter GT Championship by the end of the year.

Above: One of Butzi Porsche's finest design efforts was the clean, simple, beautiful shape of the 904, or Carrera GTS to give the car its full title.

Below: The 904 was a true dual-purpose car – here is the Scuderia Filipinetti Rey-Mercorelli car in the 1966 Alpine, pounding up a stone-covered Alpine road.

was by rack and pinion, and initially brakes and wheels were from the 356C. It was strong and heavy.

Clothing it was a body that came from the pen of Butzi Porsche, and a truly beautiful piece of work it was too. The main body panels were made for Porsche by the aircraft company Heinkel out of glass-fiber reinforced plastic, and were bonded to the steel chassis for extra stiffness and strength.

The first car was delivered in January 1964, and after the initial run of 100, Porsche laid down another batch of 20. The homologation papers had not come through in time for the 904's first race at Sebring in March, so the five that entered per-

The 904 was also Porsche's main weapon for the 1965 season and it started off remarkably well when Eugen Böhringer and Rolf Wütherich powered one through snow, ice and the usual wintry conditions to finish second in the Monte Carlo Rally. Truly the 904 seemed to be a car for all seasons. As the year before, Porsche tended to leave the GT class to private owners in their 904/4s while they concentrated on the prototype classes with 904/6s and 904/8s. At the Targa a 904/6 finished third, while at Le Mans, where once again 904s constituted the complete Porsche lineup, a 904/6 came home fourth overall and first in the Index of Performance, much to Porsche's surprise. The other 904/6 and the 904/8 retired as did, this time, the privateers.

However, back in 1962, when the 718 was dropped, there had been no real successor in the Spyder mold. That year, however, Carl Haas, an enthusiastic Speedster racer and entrepreneur, brought together Elva and Porsche. The combination of Porsche power and the ultralight, highly nimble British chassis proved highly successful in America, and the Elva-Porsche sold well. In 1965 Ferdinand Piëch took over the research and development department, and hence the racing side as well. No doubt influenced by the Elva-Porsche, he realized that the 904s, fast and strong though they were, were also too heavy. To pare off weight he ordered a Spyder body for the 904 chassis, of truly minimal dimensions, as ugly as the standard 904 was beautiful. However, looks do not win races but lightness does. Some five of these Spyders were built. A 904/8 Spyder finished second to a 3.3-liter Ferrari in the Targa in May 1965, driven by Davis and Mitter.

The European Hillclimb Championship has traditionally been important to Porsche. It takes place right on their doorstep for a start, and was limited to cars with an engine capacity of 2 liters for another. Thus, after Le Mans, Piëch and Co concentrated on the Spyders for this series. Their plans, however, were shaken quite considerably when Ludovico Scarfiotti arrived in a 2-liter Ferrari Dino, and proceeded to clean up in event after event. In something approaching desperation Piëch decided, mid-season, that a new car was needed, and fast at that. At a time when tires were growing fatter almost every day, Piëch needed 13-inch wheels for the car, similar to those on the Ferrari and Formula 1 cars of the day. Since time was too short to have some made, Piëch bought some complete with suspension components, such as uprights, from Lotus at the German Grand Prix. Out too went the 904's robust but heavy ladder chassis, replaced by a triangulated tubular space frame. In went a 2-liter flat eight, over it went a Spyder-type glass-fiber body, and the car was sent to the event for which it had been aimed: the Ollon-Villars Hillclimb in Switzerland in August. If this was a fairy tale it would have won: it didn't (the tire choice was wrong) and Scarfiotti

took the Championship. The Ollon-Villars car is important in the Porsche scheme of things to come, though.

In 1966 there was a new *Championnat International des Sport Prototypes* complete with a 2-liter

The 904 was really too bulky and heavy for sports racing, but the Elva-Porsche (*far left*) and the 718 Bergspyder showed the way to go. The 910 Bergspyder (*above*) was another pointer to the future, and came after the 906 (*below*).

class and Piëch went for it. The idea of using a 904/6 was dumped and it was decided to build a new car, given the project number 906. Homologation would require that at least 50 be made.

Thus it was that, with the 906, Piëch drew on his experience with the Ollon-Villars car. There was a space frame instead of the 904's box sections. The 904/6 did, however, provide the engine and transmission package and some of the suspension parts as well, leftovers from an aborted run of more 904s. In the engine magnesium replaced aluminum for some of the castings, and titanium replaced steel in places too. It gave a reliable 210bhp at 8000rpm. Unlike the 904, the 906 benefitted from some wind-tunnel work before it was built full-size. With its super-low nose, flared front wheel-arches, gull-wing doors and massive rear window covered in louvres it looked purposeful to put it mildly.

Come January 1966 all 50 had been sold at a list price of DM45,000, so another batch of 15 was laid down, of which nine were fitted with fuel injection and four with 2-liter flat-eight engines, so they had to run in the prototype category. The new car, officially called the Carrera 6, received its homologation on 1 May.

With only a little bit of interference from Ferrari, the 906 cleaned up in the 2-liter class of the *Championnat*. Notable victories in the process included the Targa Florio with Willy Mairesse and Herbert Müller driving. For Le Mans, two of the injected

906s and two carbureted versions were fitted with long tails (*langheck*), which, in practice, showed a remarkable ability to cause lift-off. Small trim tabs cured this and one of the injected cars, crewed by Jo Siffert and Colin Davis, finished fourth overall. In front of them was a trio of massive 7-liter Ford GT40 Mk IIs, and behind them another trio of Carrera 6s. Siffert and Davis took the Index award as well. Le Mans 1966 saw another Porsche milestone: the first 911 appeared in the race, driven by 'Franc' who with his partner Kerguen took it to 14th overall. The 911 was the only non-906 at Le Mans that year.

Almost as a sideline, 1966 also goes down as the year that the 911 emerged as a rally car: both the Osterreichische and German rallies were won by 911s. In 1967 the ever-persuasive Vic Elford joined up with Porsche, and recalled how it happened in *Old Motor* magazine:

I'll always remember having lunch with von Hanstein at the Carlton Hotel in Cannes. He said Porsche didn't have a rally programme, that it was 'a poor man's sport'. I told him Porsche had the car to win.

In the end we agreed on a rally-to-rally arrangement. My first event was the Tour of Corsica. Porsche sent over a couple of mechanics and a van: when we opened it there was nothing in it but wheels and tyres! I said, come on, most cars have something, a weak point, that breaks. Von Hanstein simply said, 'My dear chap, nothing on

Above: Vic Elford on his memorable drive to win the 1968 Monte Carlo rally.

Below: The one-piece rear deck of the 910 lifts to give access to the engine – and a lot of spare space. . . .

add lightness. The engine was basically from a 906, giving some 210bhp. The factory did not push the model and only a handful were built, though they did have their successes including firsts in the Tour de France and the Marathon again in 1969, the latter with the aid of a Sportomatic gearbox in an attempt to persuade enthusiasts that it was not really a 'soft option.'

The 911 deserves another brief spell in the spotlight. Three were fitted with very special engines, given the Type number 916, which were basically twin overhead cam conversions on the single overhead cam 911 engines, using chain drive instead of shafts and bevels as seen in previous racing engines. The Type 916 was drawn up in 1966 and first appeared in 1967. It was not a success in the 911R, but we shall hear more of it.

Elford gave Porsche another memorable victory when he won the Monte Carlo Rally in 1968 in a 911T – and the day after it finished, he flew off to America for a race the next week at Daytona in a new 907. He was one of the winning drivers there too. Vic's Monte win was repeated a year later by Bjorn Waldegaard and Lars Helmer in a 911S, with the same team scoring a hat-trick in 1970.

The period from 1966 to 1969 must have been tremendously exciting in the competitions department at Porsche. Something new seemed to appear almost every week, and engine capacities rocketed as Porsche headed for the very top. Their versatility, imagination and sheer scope of variation were quite breathtaking.

Porsches breaks.' Do you know he was right? Apart from one exception I cannot think of anything on a Porsche that has broken on me!

In 1967 Vic won the Tulip and Geneva rallies (shades of the 356) while the expatriate Pole, Sobieslav Zasada, took the Osterreichring and Polish rallies. And the team of Herrmann, Neerpasch and Elford won the Marathon de la Route in a particularly rare device, the 911R. This deceptive-looking car, to all intents and purposes a standard 911, was in fact considerably lightened, with aluminum or glass fiber replacing steel throughout, and the interior was stripped bare – even the cigarette lighter and ashtray were removed to

First in chronological order, if not in Porsche's project number sequence, was the 910. This was essentially a replacement for the Ollon-Villars car, designed to contest the Hillclimb Championship. It could take either the 911 flat six or the Type 771 flat eight, the latter with 2.0- or 2.2-liter capacity. The basic chassis was the space frame from the 906 but with extra stiffening around the engine bay, helped by bonding some of the glass-fiber outer panels to the structure. The most significant advance came in the suspension, which followed the Ollon-Villars car with 13-inch wheels, retained by a single lock-nut, and yet wider tires. There were all-new uprights and the layout of the wishbones was altered, the rear suspension aping 'state-of-the-art' Grand Prix practice. The body shape copied the 906s closely but the smaller wheels meant that the wheel-arches could be made smaller. Gull-wing doors were dropped after one flew off a 906, the roof could be removed to make a Spyder, and the vast plastic cover over the engine disappeared. The 910's drag factor was a little worse than that of the 906 but the frontal area was lower so the overall effect was about the same. There was no intention of making the 910 a customer car, but by this time Porsche had instituted a new system whereby they only ran brand-new cars in all major events, selling them afterwards to private customers. All told, some 28 of the 910 were made and at the end of 1967, when the rules governing production sports cars were changed from a requirement of 50 off to 25 off, the 910 was automatically homologated. There were *Bergspyder* versions too, specials for the hill-climbs.

For a sprint car, the 910 showed remarkable stamina. Apart from helping to win the 2-liter class in the World Championship in 1967 they were regular top-five finishers overall, invariably mixing it with the Big Ford GT40s and the Ferrari P4s. A fourth at Daytona was followed by a third at Sebring, another third at Monza, a second at Spa, and then two firsts at the Targa, with two youngsters, Paul Hawkins and Rolf Stommelen driving, and the Nürburgring 1000 kms, with Joe Buzetta and Udo Schütz taking the honors. At Le Mans a six-cylinder 910 finished sixth, and the model formed the basis for their attack on the hills. Either Stommelen or Mitter won all those that counted towards the championship.

However, barely was the ink dry on the design of the 910, when another sports racer appeared as if by magic from Piëch and his men. Designated the 907 in an attempt to get back into the correct numbering sequence (quite where 910 came from seems to have been a mystery) it was intended for Le Mans rather than the hillclimbs. To this end it sported a body that was the result of considerable research at the Stuttgart Technical Institute wind tunnel. To compensate for a shorter nose than the 910 there was a very long tail. *Langheck* by heck was right ... There was a much narrower glass house, too, to try and overcome some of the disadvantages of the extra frontal area of the latest

Below: The 910's lines were clearly derived from those of the 906.

Left: The 907L could reach a top speed close on 190mph with an engine of only 2 liters.

super-wide tires. The 907s, incidentally, were all right-hand-drive cars, the first racing Porsches to be so equipped: left-hand-drive on clockwise circuits (which most are) did not really make sense so this was an overdue change.

Two 907Ls (*Langheck*) were sent to Le Mans for the practice days in April 1967. This proved that the cars may cleave through the air with the greatest of ease, but that stability while doing so was notably lacking – it is said that the drivers didn't dare take their hands off the wheel to change gear into top. The shape was tweaked a little for the Le Mans race, and it would be nice to report that the 907L won at Le Mans in 1967, but this was the great year of the Ford-Ferrari duel, with seven of each marque contesting the lead. Nevertheless, the Siffert/Herrmann 907L finished fifth overall, took the 2-liter class and the Index of Performance. The Stommelen/Neerpasch 910 was sixth, and the Elford/Pon 906 seventh, which showed the niceties of age if nothing else. For Le Mans the 907 was fitted with the 911 six, but for its only other appearance that year, at Brands in July, there was a Type 771 eight, and a much shorter, more wieldy tail.

Opposition at Daytona in February 1968 consisted mainly of the John Wyer-run Gulf GT40s, but they fell by the way and it was 907Ls with 2.2-liter eights under that long plastic rear window which romped home in first, second and third positions. To rub it in, they crossed the line in line-abreast formation, while the winning car had been driven by no less than five drivers: Elford and Neerpasch who had started in it, and Siffert, Herrmann and Stommelen whose drives had disappeared through accidents and breakdowns. For Sebring the tails were chopped off and Messrs Siffert and Herrmann promptly won, trailed by Elford and Neerpasch in another 907, the latter somewhat the worse for wear.

The results list for the Targa show that Elford and the veteran Maglioli won the event. What they do not show is that Elford lost considerable time through a wheel coming adrift. When this was repaired he drove the race of a lifetime, aided by the veteran Maglioli, and with a series of record-shattering laps hauled in the leading Alfa to win. After the Targa, though, Porsche switched their attention to yet another new model, the 908.

The 908 arose because of what can only be described as a brainstorm by the CSI (now the FIA): they changed the rules of sports-car racing. What's more, they only gave the manufacturers six months' notice, a clear breach of their own regulations. Henceforth prototypes would be limited to 3.0 liters and limited-production cars to 5 liters with a minimum of 50 off. There had been threats that Ford, having won Le Mans with the mighty 7-liter Mk IIs would pull out: this they did. Possibly a bigger blow, though, was that Enzo Ferrari did exactly the same thing. Other losses included the Chaparral and the Lola-Aston Martin. Which left pretty few runners: Porsche, obviously: Alfa Romeo, too; and the possibility of Matra and Renault, both French companies – was it coincidence that the CSI was based in France?

Piëch and his men reviewed the matter calmly. The 907 had proved itself throughout 1967, and on the slower circuits had given the big boys a run for their money. What was needed was more power, which a 3-liter would provide. But which engine? The Type 771 2.2-liter eight could not be enlarged that far, and besides which was complex and expensive. On top of that, Ferry Porsche put a clamp on spending: the 907 had shown signs of running away with costs. One promising avenue was that twin-cam conversion of the 911 that had been tried earlier, the Type 916. Adding two cylinders sounds difficult but in reality was not, and it would bring it up to capacity. On top of that, with chain

Top right, and center right: The 907 was essentially a more aerodynamic version of the 910, with a lower drag factor and less frontal area.

Right: Long- and short-tailed 906s sandwich a Ferrari at Mulsanne during the 1966 Le Mans race.

drive at the front and using much 911 technology, it would be a relatively cheap and simple engine. To cope with the extra torque, there was a new and beefy six-speed transaxle, but it proved troublesome and drivers did not take to the change pattern, so it was later replaced with a five-speed box.

The 908 was both the biggest and most powerful engine Porsche had ever made up till then, giving 310bhp on initial tests but some 350bhp by the time it appeared in a car. It was only the fifth major engine change they had made. However, it was not the instant success its predecessors had been and in its first year proved something of a dis-appointment. But it more than made up for this in following years. It started off badly, too: at the traditional Le Mans test day the new car, like the 907L, proved terrifyingly unstable – and it was travelling at 190mph on the Mulsanne straight. In the first race in which 908s raced, at Monza, they disappointed, finishing way, way back. For the 'Ring, a month later, the long tails had been chopped off and two 908Ks (for *Kurzheck* meaning short tail) were entered. Siffert and Elford won but that was the 908's only major victory that year.

When the 908s came to Watkins Glen in July they were all Ks, but with a difference: they were fitted with movable flaps on the tail which were connected to, and operated by, the suspension. As the car rolled in a corner, the inner flap attached to the inner hub rose as the wheel rose, thus providing downforce where it was needed.

Above: Although the 917 was strictly a two-seater to meet the regulations, the passenger was given very little space!

Similarly underbraking the tail would lift, the flaps rise in sympathy, and thus press the tail down again, adding to the braking effects. Alas, in spite of such clever ideas (which would subsequently be banned as 'movable aerodynamic devices') only one 908 finished and that down in sixth place.

Potentially, Le Mans 1968 was the year that Porsche could pull off the dream: win Le Mans. They had the car, the 908, and time since the race had been postponed from its usual date in June to September because of student riots. The four works cars were all 908s, with three private 907s and assorted other Porsches as backup. Siffert and Herrmann led for the first three hours. They had a two-lap lead when they retired. All the 908s had problems and only one finished, third behind the Rodriguez/Bianchi GT40 and the Squadra Tartaruga 907 driven by Spoerry and Steinemann.

In January 1969 Porsche rolled out the cars for that year. There were three versions of the 908, L, K and a Spyder, the last designed to take advantage of a change in rules that governed prototypes with engines up to 3 liters – they were no longer required to have a minimum ground clearance, windshield height or room for a suitcase and spare wheel. Porsche, therefore, removed the roof of the 908 and the 908/02 was born.

Also on show was a real rarity, a 909. This was an ultralight (450 kg) hillclimb special, whose fea-

tures included a gearbox in front of the differential and an incredibly short wheelbase, which meant that the driver was pushed so far forward his feet projected out in front of the axle center line. There was also a novel fuel system: the tank was a pressurized sphere which in theory did away with fuel pumps and other non-essentials, but in practice it did not work so was abandoned. The 909 only raced twice, at Gaisberg and Mont Ventoux, driven by Rolf Stommelen, and was beaten on each occasion by Mitter in a 910. Its importance lies in the fact that, like the Ollon-Villars car, it was a pointer to the future.

There was a hesitant start to 1969 with the 908s. At Daytona all five retired. At Sebring a Spyder, having its first race, finished third. But, from then on, 1969 was the year of the 908. They took the first three places in the BOAC 500 at Brands Hatch, the first four at the Targa, and the first five no less at the 'Ring – a clear case of overkill. One of the 908s was fitted with a new, more aerodynamic body, with a less dramatic 'coke bottle' curvature: because of its simplicity and its flatness it was nicknamed the Sole.

Perhaps the 908's greatest moment, though, was when one came second. It was at Le Mans in 1969. A 917, making its first appearance at the Sarthe circuit, led comfortably for much of the race but retired on Sunday morning. On the whole, Pors-

che was having a miserable time of it, with both 917s, two 908 coupés and the 908/02 falling by the wayside. That only left the Herrmann/Larrousse 908 still in with a chance, and gradually the Frenchman pulled in the leader, the Gulf Ford being driven by Jackie Oliver. Herrmann and Ickx took over for the final stint, and put on a display of motor racing usually only seen on the first lap of a Grand Prix, the veteran of 13 Le Mans faster on top speed but the Belgian youngster with a slight advantage underbraking and cornering. At the line the Ford was ahead of the Porsche, but only just. It left drivers, teams and spectators exhausted, and the 908 became instantly immortal.

Like so many of its forebears, the 908 had a long and illustrious life in private hands. For example, one of the cars in the Watkins Glen race, a 908/02 (the Sole) was bought by an Englishman, Tony Dean, who was following the Canadian-American (Can-Am) series. He would go down in the Porsche annals as the first Porsche driver to win one of these races, at Road Atlanta in 1970.

Nor did Porsche rest the 908 on its laurels. Since the mighty 917 might prove just a little too mighty for such tortuous circuits as the Targa or the Nürburgring, they produced the 908/03. This was, in effect, an offshoot of that ugly and rather ineffectual hillclimb car, the 909. Like the 909, the gearbox was placed between engine and differential and the driver was pushed right up into the nose. With its major masses in the middle it had a very low polar moment of inertia which meant it was incredibly responsive, a quality which would be needed on sinuous tracks. Obligingly, a 908/03 won the Targa in 1970, and the Nürburgring 1000 kms in both 1970 and 1971.

Above: Enormously evocative – 917s in Gulf colors gave the world some of the finest racing ever seen.

Below: The 917's shape was decreed more by aerodynamic stability than efficiency, hence the curious bodywork around the tail.

but by heaven it was efficient and the shape would be picked up later for some 917 Spyders.

Of course, 908/03s were offered to customers and they continued to provide good backup to the 917s and, when the 917s were eventually forced off the circuits by the rule-makers, they carried on after them. In fact, one of the most remarkable must be that of Reinhold Jöst. In the mid-1970s it was fitted with a 2.1-liter turbocharged flat six giving some 450bhp (with factory help) and it appeared regularly as recently as 1980. By then, of course, it bore very little resemblance to the early 908s but there was a direct, lineal, continuous history to the car, making it one of the longest-lived competitive machines ever.

Unfortunately for the 908, its thunder would be stolen by an even more thunderous device, arguably the most exciting and certainly the most powerful racing car to date – the mighty 917. The 917 was the result of the same glorious cockup that saw the 908 arrive, that decision by the CSI to limit prototype to 3 liters and Group 4 production cars to 5 liters with a 50-off run. Intended to give the Ford and Chevrolet powered cars a sporting chance, the 5-liter limit was acceptable, but the 50 off was not. There was no way that Lola and the others could run up and sell 50 such cars. After some bickering between the CSI and the manufacturers, the figure was brought down to 25 in April 1968. The CSI, of course, thought they were implementing a rule which would simply allow the old big bangers a final fling instead of making

The body shape of the 908/03 was as different as it could possibly be. Blunt-nosed, slab-sided, flat-topped with openings for driver, fuel injection and cooling and with knife-edged fender tops, it was as ugly as some of the others had been beautiful

Right: 908s were tough! Gerhard Koch 'yumps' a 908/02 at the Nürburgring in 1969. He retired. . . .

Left: Some 600bhp was a tight fit in the 917's tail – and note the 'get you home' spare!

Below: Awesome! The Stommelen/ Ahrens 917 was stunningly fast at Le Mans in 1969 – while it lasted.

Above: The 908/02 was basically a Spyder version of the 908 coupé.

Below: The 908/03, on the other hand, was designed to be as compact as possible and damn the aerodynamics. Look closely and you'll see that Elford has all four wheels off the ground – in mid-corner!

From July 1968 on Piëch and his team worked on the 917, using the Porsche project number Type 912 to disguise their efforts, and within nine months the car was ready. Chassis design drew heavily on that of the 908, not surprisingly, being an aluminum tubular space frame suitably adapted: this at a time, remember, when Ford and Lola had proved the idea of a monocoque tub. Suspension was by fully adjustable, 'state-of-the-art' wishbones and coils at each corner.

Adding another four cylinders to the 908's flat eight would give 4.5 liters, enough to be getting on with they decided, so the new flat-twelve engine to power the 917 used the same con-rod length, valve and port sizes and bore and stroke as the 908s. However, simply adding four more pots to the 908 would have been impractical since it would have produced an unacceptably long and whippy crankshaft. So they reverted to Type 771 thinking: the engine would be made in two halves, with both valve and power drive being taken from the center. Thus the crankshaft was split amidships with a central gear meshing with the output shaft beneath it and the valve gear train on either side (Porsche opted for gears rather than shafts as heretofore – memories of the complexities of the Type 547 lingered). Heads were as per the Type 916, with two valves per cylinder, on paper an anachronistic move when four valves per cylinder were the norm. However, there was justification for such a setup: with all those cooling

them obsolete overnight, and that the 3-liter prototypes would take over. But then for some time Porsche had been building new cars for any important race, finding it no more expensive than maintaining a smaller fleet, and reducing the risk of fatigue failures. A run of 25 pure racers not only wasn't a problem, they might well build that many anyway. And then, of course, there were stories, later justified, that Ferrari had seen the 25-off loophole, and was planning a series of cars for Group 4 (the Ferrari 512, one of the few that could give a 917 a run for its money). Ferry Porsche, egged on by Ferdinand Piëch, decided to give the project a chance.

fins there was not room for four valves, and in any case the first flat twelve gave 542bhp on the bench when tested. Enough was enough, and there was more, much more, to come if it was needed. A new five-speed gearbox was developed as well to take the 376lb ft of torque the engine produced.

The chassis weighed a mere 104 lb, and had one unusual feature: it was pressurized. If a pressure gauge was connected to it a check could be made to see if there were any cracks in it: a drop in pressure indicated a leak and, therefore, a crack. The body (the original weighed only 83 lb) was similar to the 908s but was developed separately – it was no carbon copy. And each 917 would come with a choice of tails, long or short.

To say the 917 created a sensation when it was unveiled at Geneva in March 1969 is an understatement – an uproar would be more like it. Obviously the fastest thing on four wheels for the track, it stunned all those who saw it – and the members of the CSI who had to homologate it. Porsche rubbed it in by handing out catalogues for the car, pricing it at DM140,000.

There had been some muttering within the ranks that some of the Group 4 constructors were being a little casual about the number of cars they had made, so when the inspectors from the CSI

went to look at the cars to homologate them toward the end of March they refused to accept a few cars and piles of bits. On their return on 21 April they were greeted with 25 pristine, immaculate, complete 917s, neatly lined up outside the factory. I once asked Dean Delamont, one of the two CSI representatives there that day what his reactions were, and he just shrugged and then said, 'We couldn't say much could we? Especially when one of the Porsche people, absolutely deadpan, handed us a box of keys and asked us if we'd like to choose one and take it out, just to prove they weren't dummies!' It had taken Porsche ten months to design and build 25 examples of one of the greatest racing cars ever.

Above: Two Porsche greats, Jo Siffert and Pedro Rodriguez, trying to outbrake each other in 908/03s.

Below: The *Langheck* 908 coupé was used for the faster, long-distance races.

All the drivers loved the idea of the car but driving it was another matter. If there had been problems with the 910 and the 907, the 917 with all its extra horsepower was a different breed of animal altogether. Elford and Siffert tried the car at Spa and scared themselves deeply. Mitter drove one in the race but fortunately for him blew it on the first lap. In spite of its fearsome reputation, earned very, very rapidly, some drivers were prepared to take it on, and Elford and another Englishman, Richard Attwood, put a 917 into a huge lead at Le Mans in 1969 before an oil seal went. With relatively narrow tires and suspension that suffered from high camber changes, not to mention decidedly odd aerodynamics, the 917

Below: The famous line-up of 917s, ready for FIA inspection.

had to be approached with caution. One of the 917s was timed at 236mph along the Mulsanne straight (20mph faster than anything ever before) but tragedy struck very early on when John Woolfe, a talented but not spectacular private owner who bought the first customer 917, lost control on the opening lap and was killed as the car smashed into the barrier. The first victory of the 917 came at the Osterreichring 1000 kms with Siffert and Ahrens driving.

Porsche's main opposition the year before , in 1968, had come from the Gulf sponsored JW Automotive team, headed by John Wyer, of GT40s. These were rapidly becoming obsolete – especially in view of the 917 – while Porsche were

Right: The SERA-designed long-tail body for the 917.

finding the effort of doing absolutely everything themselves, from designing, building, developing to racing, costly both financially and in terms of manpower. A logical step would be to draw someone like the JW setup into the net to look after the administration and the racing for the 1970 and 1971 seasons, while Porsche would supply cars and technology. An agreement was duly signed, but Wyer was a little perturbed to find that a similar agreement had been reached with Porsche-Salzburg, Louise Piëch's operation in Austria. (In 1971 the Austrian team changed hands to become Martini Racing, headed by Willi Kauhsen.) Wyer's team, however, had a bonus for they dealt directly with the Stuttgart experimental department, while all the others, Porsche-Salzburg included, had to use the racing service department.

A cure to the car's instability problems had to be found rapidly, and it was. Both Porsche and JW had raced at the Osterreichring, before any agreement had been signed, and together ran some extended tests on the 917. David Yorke, team manager for JW, noted that there were not any squashed bugs on the car's long and curvy tail – obviously, it was not giving much if any downforce. There and then, using the pit barrier as a body former (and rather to the horror of the Porsche technicians who were present) his men snipped and beat out an aluminum sheet, attached it to the tail of a 917K, and the results were more than promising. (At the same session was the Spyder version of the 917, the 917PA – PA standing for Porsche + Audi – a hesitant start at a potential Can-Am machine. Interestingly, it handled much better than the coupés.)

The new-shape 917s first appeared at Daytona late in January 1970. Gulf entered two cars, Porsche-Salzburg one. They were fitted with a novel tweak – small windows above the main windshield. These allowed the drivers to see where they were going, for at a banking such as that at Daytona the road appears to the drivers to curve both up and around. The 917 made a good start to the year, the Gulf cars finishing 1-2, the Porsche-Salzburg car retiring.

From then on there was no holding them. Ferrari tried with the glorious 512 but of the 24 Championship races for which the 917 was entered from 1969 through 1971 it won 15, and 908s won another four, which left Porsche beaten on only five occasions. No fewer than 36 Ks, 2 Spyders and 5 Ls were built, rather more than the requirements – perhaps Porsche could even have built the 50 as originally required.

At Le Mans in 1970 there were seven 917s lined up. Gulf brought 3 Ks, two of which were fitted with the 4.9-liter engine which had appeared at Monza shortly before. Two others from Porsche-Salzburg were long-tails, one with a 4.9-liter engine for Elford and Ahrens (backed up by a K for Herrmann and Attwood), the other a 4.5-liter long-tail with the most eye-catching color-scheme devised, very tongue-in-cheek, by Tony Lapine's studio (it consisted of purple and green flames). The sixth was a K entered and driven by David Piper and Gijs van Lennep.

Below: A real rarity –the Type 909 Hillclimb special at Gaisberg, Austria.

The race itself turned out to be less than fantastic, with plenty of rain and many retirements including all the Gulf cars and the Elford/Ahrens Porsche-Salzburg machine. In fact, it was the second-string Herrmann/Attwood car that got the mixture between speed and stamina right and finished first, giving Porsche the result they had always dreamed of – a victory at Le Mans. Herrmann, after 14 Le Mans races, retired on the spot too. In second place was the colorful Martini car.

The record that year, 1970, shows the JW cars taking Daytona, the BOAC 500 at Brands Hatch, the Monza 1000 kms, the Targa Florio (in a 908/03 though), Watkins Glen 6 Hours, Imola, the Osterreichring 1000 kms and the Kyalami 9 Hours, honors going to Porsche-Salzburg at the Nürburgring and Le Mans. The only championship round they did not win was the Sebring 12 Hours.

Just in case the Ferraris should prove troublesome in 1971, Porsche designed and built a 16-cylinder engine for the season, but they needn't have bothered. Ferrari had plumped for the 3-liter prototype category with his 312s, leaving the big 5-liter machines in private hands. However, Alfa Romeo with their T33/3s proved thorny at times, and defeated the Porsche battalions three times, at Brands, Watkins Glen and, most embarrassingly, at the Targa Florio. Nevertheless, the Porsches, by dint of furious in-fighting between the two major teams Gulf and Martini (ex-Porsche-Salzburg), put up some excellent racing.

Right: Porsche people: (left to right) Paul Hawkins, Jo Siffert, Hans Herrmann and Kurt Ahrens after a Porsche 1-2 at Zeltweg in 1968.

Below: Pit action at Le Mans. Siffert (left) heads down the lane, hands in pockets, while David Yorke hurries around the nose of the car.

The expected results came at Buenos Aires and Daytona with Gulf taking the honors in 4.9-liter cars. Elford and Larrousse in a Martini car won at Sebring, and then at Brands Siffert and a newcomer to the Gulf team, Derek Bell, won with a full 5-liter (in fact 4999cc).

For Le Mans Gulf took two long-tails for Rodriguez/Oliver and Siffert/Bell, backing them with a short-tail for Attwood and Müller. Martini had a long-tail for Elford and Larrousse and a short-tail for van Lennep and Marko, plus another very curious device indeed. Designed in the SERA wind tunnel in Paris as an attempt at a low-drag body, it looked gross – so much so that Tony Lapine and his team painted it pink and turned it into a butcher's diagram for the cuts of pork. Naturally, it was called the Pink Pig.

In the race Rodriguez and Elford made the running to start with, but then the Elford car dropped out, followed around the halfway mark by all the Gulf cars – a Ferrari 512 led at half distance. At the finish, though, the Marko/van Lennep Martini car led the Attwood/Müller car across the line, all the other 917s having dropped out.

From then on the long-distance 917 program slowly wound down as the cars came to the end of

their useful life – in World Championship races at least. A win at Zeltweg in Austria saw Porsche clinch the title for the second year running. The 917's life in one form of racing had been a short couple of years, though Porsche had foreseen this since the 5-liter limit had only ever been intended to keep other cars going for a little longer – no one expected Porsche to react so positively and rapidly as they did. That foulup by the powers-that-be led to some of the greatest cars and races ever. Sadly, two of the best 917 drivers lost their lives in 1971 in other makes, Rodriguez and Siffert.

In fact, it had been Siffert who had been inspir-ational in Porsche mounting a toe-hold operation in 1969 in another branch of sports-car racing, the Can-Am series across the Atlantic. Eschewing 3-liter limits (the Americans didn't make engines that small) they had devised Can-Am as a sort of homebrewed sports-racing series with minimal rules as far as engine capacity and weight were concerned. The result was some spectacular cars – every bit as spectacular as the 917s – usually built by small concerns like McLaren and Lola, and with massive 7- and 8-liter engines. Could the 917 be adapted perhaps? The creation of the Pors-che + Audi setup there saw pressure applied.

Above: First – at last. Porsche's very first overall win at Le Mans came in 1970, the Porsche-Salzburg 917K being driven by Hans Herrmann and Dickie Attwood.

Left: The amazing SERA-designed 917 at Le Mans, 1971. The Porsche styling department painted it pink with assorted cuts of pork on it! Hence the nickname of 'Pink Pig.'

Porsche profiles:
1. 1969 4.5 L
2. 1969 4.5 K
3. 1969 4.5 Can-Am
4. 1969 K modified tail
5. 1970 4.5 K
6. 1970 4.9 L
7. 1971 4.9 K.

Their first efforts were with the 917PA, or 917 Spyder, as mentioned earlier. Since the 917 long-distance program took up so much time in 1969, the 917PA did not appear until late in the season (it was given the curious racing number 0) and, with Ritchie Ginther as team manager, Jo Siffert put up some good displays, eventually taking fourth overall in the championship. As set up originally it was ultrasmooth, but it soon became clear that the tighter circuits used in Can-Am called for down-force, more downforce and yet more downforce. Thus it was not very long before the 917PA started growing spoilers all over the place, two vast ear-like probosces at the front and billboard-sized flat plates at the back.

Porsche took a sabbatical year in Can-Am in 1970 but toward the end of the year interest in Can-Am was reactivated. Very nearly as important in this context was another new series of races, the Interserie, based mainly in Germany but encompassing other countries in Europe as well. The purpose behind Interserie was to do for 917 owners what the 5-liter formula had done for GT40 owners – prevent their viciously expensive cars becoming obsolete overnight. It was not of world championship status, but 917s, and 917 Spyders in particular, were regular competitors and winners while it was in operation.

Thus it was that, in the winter of 1970, a new design of 917 Spyder was put in hand. Called the 917/10, it naturally used most of the 917's components, including engine, chassis and running gear, but clothed in a new body. Much closer to the final variant of the 917PA and 908/03 than to either the K or L, it featured a wedge-shaped nose with the oil cooler imposed on top, while the center and rear sections rose gently to the stubby tail, with fins each side. It was notably wider than the standard 917s too, to cover vast tires. To give more power, the engine capacity was increased to 5347cc which in turn gave a useful 660bhp but that was no

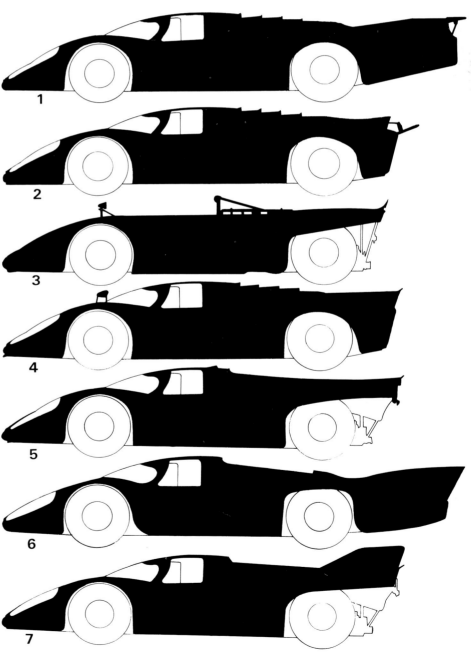

Right: Imagine the thunder! The glorious start to Le Mans in 1971, the Porsches and Ferraris already at each others' throats.

Bottom right: The 917 Spyder, forerunner of the Can-Am cars, under test.

Porsche profiles:
8. 1971 4.9 L
9. 1971 4.9 K
10. 1971 5.0 Can-Am
11. 1972 5.4 Can-Am
12. 1972 917/10
13. 1973 917/30

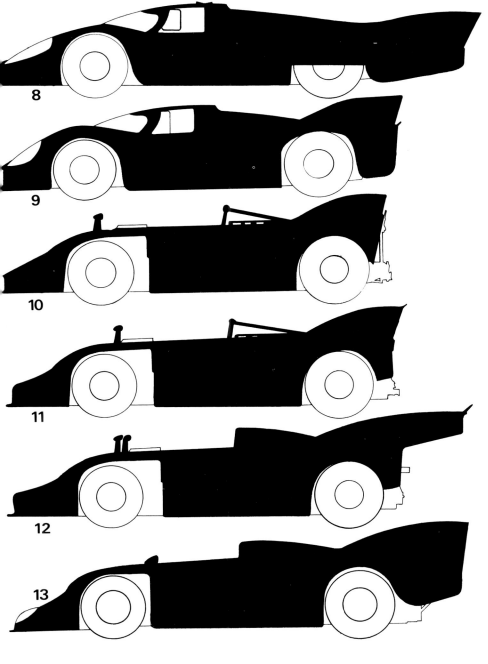

8

9

10

11

12

13

match for the 780bhp of the McLaren-Chevrolets. Still, Siffert obtained some sponsorship from Marlboro and STP (this was very much a private venture, albeit factory-aided) and, with a 5-liter engine, while the bigger unit was being built, he went to America. In six rounds he was never lower than fifth place, but was then killed at Brands Hatch and that was the end of Can-Am as far as Porsche was concerned in 1971.

The slow-down in effort in mid-1971 on the long-distance front allowed Porsche to concentrate more on Can-Am. There was one important issue to be decided though: who was to run the team. Porsche themselves knew comparatively little about Can-Am but there was one team who had an enormous reputation in America: Roger Penske's outfit. Talks between the two sides culminated in an announcement in November that Roger Penske Racing would run Porsche cars in the 1972 Can-Am series, the cars being 917/10s. One of Penske's strengths was his driver, Mark Donohue, who was not only a very fast driver but a brilliant engineer who could sort out cars properly. Donohue spent much time at Weissach, tuning the 917/10 to his exacting requirements. One car, fitted with a 5-liter engine, was freighted out to America in December 1971 for testing on American tracks, where it proved disappointing.

Above: Early days in Can-Am – Jo Siffert in the 917PA.

Right: The late, great, Jo Siffert.

However, Porsche had another weapon up their sleeve. They could increase the power on the engine by making it bigger (but not by very much – 5.4 liters was the limit with safety) or supercharge it. Turbochargers, in which the exhaust gases drive a little turbine which in turn drives an impeller which is used to compress the in-going air, were the darlings of engine engineers in the early 1970s. They offered what everyone wanted – something for nothing. Porsche, as a research and development company, were naturally *au fait* with developments and had been experimenting with turbo-blowers for a couple of years. Why not turbocharge the flat twelve?

By January 1972 their efforts were sufficiently advanced for a blown 4.5-liter engine to be sent to America. It gave 800-plus bhp without problems. Well, without problems on the test bench: in practice both drivers and Porsche were discovering such factors as turbo lag followed by instant response as the turbo cut in. Trial and error saw the problems diminished to the point where its drivability was just about acceptable. Then, when a turbocharger was fitted to a full 5-liter engine, there were flash readings of 1000bhp. That should be quite enough to see off the powerful big-block American engines.

Above: Battle-scarred. The winning Rodriguez/Kinnunen 917K at Daytona, 1970. Note the additional 'window' above the windshield so the drivers could see where they were going on the banking!

Right: The prototype 917/10 snapped, all unsuspectingly, by Doug Nye at Weissach in 1972. Away from public eyes the Porsche technicians didn't care what the cars looked like, and stuck various aerodynamic addenda all over the place. The vertical front fins didn't make it to the track.

Right: The amazing technicolor 917.

Below: The future World Champion, Jody Scheckter, drove Vasek Polak's 917/10 in 1973.

Left: Rodriguez and Oliver won the 1971 Monza 1000 Kms fairly easily.

Attention was also paid to the suspension, running gear and bodywork. With so much power available, it was all too easy to spin an inside rear wheel even with a limited slip differential in action. Tests on the Weissach skid-pan proved that, in fact, locking the diff solid gave the best handling – so the diff was simply removed. As for aerodynamics, a huge wing sprouted up at the back, supported by fins either side. To counteract the downforce this produced, there was a new nose, with concave wing ending in a flat tray near enough at ground level, with the oil cooler mounted on a boxy structure between them.

A minor fault relegated Donohue to second place in the 917/10's first race at Mosport, and then, in practice for the Road Atlanta Race, the whole rear deck came adrift, causing Donohue to suffer a massive accident. This more or less put him out of action for the rest of the year, but George Follmer stepped into his seat in the L&M sponsored car. So well had it been developed that Follmer fairly easily won five races and took the 1972 Can-Am Championship. Porsche made a few other 917/10s that year, but they were kitted out either with the unblown 5.0s or blown 4.5s – Penske were the only ones to run blown 5.0s all season.

Porsche and Penske returned to Can-Am for another year, and in the process annihilated everything in sight. Their weapon was the ultimate 917, and many say the ultimate racer – the 917/30, of which only two were made. They were, in fact, almost a brand-new design, with extra length but

Above: The magnificent 917/30 in full flight, using all its 1100bhp.

Right: George Follmer took over the 917/10 in 1972 and emerged as Can-Am champion.

less width. There was a more rounded nose, designed by SERA, and a longer tail, at the end of which was a wing of truly vast proportions. And, in that lengthy tail, there was the ultimate engine: a turbocharged 5.4-liter, delivering a regular 1100bhp though flash readings of 1500bhp and more were seen in the test cells. As ever, it was immaculately finished, this time in Sunoco blue, yellow and red colors.

There were two retirements in 1973 in the first two races, caused by an accident and a fuel leak respectively, but that was the only time the 917/30 put a foot wrong. The only opposition came from other Porsches, 917/10s in the hands of George Follmer and Jody Scheckter, but for the other six races Donohue won by the proverbial country mile.

Pressure from other competitors saw the rules change for Can-Am in 1974, so the 917/30 was honorably retired, unbeaten after only one year. But what a car! Surely the ghost of the Professor must have been chuckling to see it thunder round the circuits, just as another of his designs with the driver placed far forward and a huge engine behind him, had done in the 1930s. The name Porsche links two of the finest racing machines ever seen, the Auto Union and the mighty 917. Surely the Professor has much to be proud about.

Left: With the Porsche withdrawal from sports-car racing it was left to privateers to uphold Porsche honors in the mid-1970s: this is a 908/03 at Silverstone in 1974.

Below: Even as late as 1980 the 908 was competitive. This is Sigi Brunn at Brands Hatch in 1980.

DOMINATION ON THE TRACKS

Above: The 911 soldiered on for years as a competitive rally car – this one is taking part in the Monte Carlo Rally in 1983.

Previous pages: The 'Fuhrmann philosophy' – to race cars based on production 911s – was highly successful, as evinced by a pair of 935s at Silverstone in 1979 (pursued by an elderly 908!)

From 1973 on, the 917s had been effectively banned from any major international world-class championships, and were, therefore, retired to rest on their laurels. Porsche had put much time, effort and money into the 917 program, too much to just close up shop and steal quietly away. Where to turn next, though? With Ferdinand Piëch gone, much of the impetus, and not a little of the ability, for such racing had gone too. The disruption of the changes at the top elsewhere didn't help. Then there were those falling sales in 1970 and 1971. Ernst Fuhrmann pondered over these and other matters in his first year of office, and came to a conclusion not dissimilar to that which Ferry had reached back in the early 1960s after the F1 and F2 episodes. A return to basics was needed. With the 911 there was the raw material to branch out into other directions, but with a car which was instantly identifiable to everyone as a Porsche. Enter the 'Fuhrmann philosophy.'

The 911 formed a good basis with which to start. Driven by such stalwarts as Elford, Zasada, Waldegard and Toivonen, it had scored some outstanding rally successes, including the European Rally Drivers Championship in 1968 and 1970. In racing too it was beginning to earn a name for itself: in 1967 at Le Mans, only the second year a 911 had taken part, an S entered by Veuillet, the entrant for that very first Porsche back in 1951, came second in the GT category. In 1972 John Fitzpatrick, driving Erwin Kremer's 911S, won the European GT Championship by a huge margin. The potential was there.

It would obviously need a lot of work on it to make it competitive in the higher echelons of the sport and not just class wins. If it was going to combat the big Ferraris and De Tomasos, it would have to have more power for starters. To make the power even more effective it would have to lose weight, and to make the power and loss of weight still more effective yet it would have to go around corners a lot faster.

The first attempt in this direction was an instant success: the Carrera RS 2.7. With the 2.7-liter

engine and the deletion of anything that was not necessary, plus fatter tires under those distinctive bulged wheel-arches, the Carrera 2.7 made a sensational road car, and a pretty good track car. However, the regulations governing the GT Championship allowed certain changes to be made to the engine and suspension for the track. The RS was just the raw material: for the racing version, the RSR, Porsche most certainly pulled out all the stops.

Opening up the bore as much as was feasible at the time gave 2806cc. Other modifications such as twin plug heads saw an easy 300bhp at 8000rpm on the dyno. The rules allowed an extra 2 inches on wheel-arch width and any size of tire so long as they fitted under those arches: on went those wider arches and in them went wheels that were 9 inches wide at the front and 11 inches wide at the rear. One instant distinguishing point of the RSR was the large oil cooler in the nose, under the center of the bumper.

The homologation papers for the RS did not come into effect until March 1973, but by then the RSR had already claimed its first victory. Running in the prototype class at the Daytona 24 hours, up against full-bore racers such as the Matras, Mirages and Lolas, an RSR driven by Peter Gregg and Hurley Haywood won outright. In fact, a bitter battle had developed during the race between the Penske RSR, driven by Donohue and Follmer, and the Gregg/Haywood Brumos machine, resolved when a piston went on the Penske car.

For 1973, Porsche on the whole left it to privateers to contest the GT Championship, as they had done with the 904s, and indeed such stalwarts as the Kremer team and Gelo Racing proved more than adequate. Porsche themselves started to explore the 911 dynamic envelope and to that end contented themselves with just two cars, Martini-backed, but entered in the prototype class. One of the biggest changes was a further increase in capacity, to 2994cc, which was to lead to a comment by Ferry Porsche that, had he known when the flat six was designed that it could be progressively enlarged he would have insisted that it be scaled down. However, in order to achieve the extra capacity, an aluminum crankcase was necessary – on the surface a retrograde step since it was heavier, but the bigger bore holes meant there was precious little space left between them, and aluminum was stronger. With special heads, the 3.0-liter gave 315bhp. Suspension and aerodynamics came in for treatment too, and eventually the Martini-Carreras were fitted with massive wheels and tires from the 917, 10.5 inches wide at the front and 15 inches wide at the rear. Then there were huge rear spoilers which wrapped around the edges of the tail and blended into the ultrawide rear fenders. In this form a Martini-Carrera won the last of the Targa Florios on the Little Madonie circuit, beating the prototype Ferraris and Alfas in the process. A more fitting winner couldn't be imagined.

Above: The first appearance, and first victory, of the Carrera at Daytona 1973 driven by Gregg and Haywood.

Right: Porsche tried very hard indeed to win the East African Safari rally but never quite made it. . . .

The success of the Carrera RS in sales terms – about 1600 were built – meant that it qualified for Group 3, a normal production car. To stay in Group 3 only required a limited run of 100, so Porsche built 109 Carrera RS 3.0s and this allowed the racing version, the RSR, to fall into Group 4 with a full 3-liter engine. For 1974 the RSRs followed the Martini cars of the year before, with 917-type wheels fore and aft, and an engine that gave about 330bhp. Visually they were noticeable because of the way the fiber-glass fenders draped over the wheels: at the front they simply ended at the door leaving a gaping hole, and at the back there were large air intakes fore and aft. There was also a clutch of special Carreras, halfway between RSs and RSRs. Fifteen were built for Roger Penske for the 1974 International Race of Champions, a four-race series for the big names of motor racing. Donohue walked away with it, pocketing over $50,000 in the process.

The company did not race any of the RSR 3.0s, leaving that to their customers. And they repaid Porsche's confidence: in 1974 they won the IMSA Championship, the European GT Championship, the FIA GT Cup and a whole string of other major successes – then repeated the same performance in 1975.

However, in September 1973 Porsche displayed what looked perilously like a dream car on their stand at Frankfurt: the 911 Turbo. At the same time they announced that they were cutting back on their racing activities, but would, with Martini backing again, enter a turbocharged Carrera in Group 5 in the World Championship of Makes in 1974. As in 1973, this set an upper limit of 3 liters unblown, which reduced by a factor of 1.4 if a turbocharger was fitted. (There were also rumors that, as from 1976, the World Championship of Makes would be for Group 5 production-based machines, which of course suited the 'Fuhrmann philosophy' perfectly.)

Thus the 2.14-liter Turbo Carrera came into being, the odd capacity coming from the

equivalency factor. The engine reverted to a magnesium crankcase since just over 2 liters was well within its limits. The bore was special, 83mm, between that of the 2.0- and 2.2-liter 911 units. A KKK turbocharger was used, and fed the engine via an air-to-air intercooler, which increased charge density for more power, and reduced engine temperatures for longer life. It also gave a stunning 450bhp, give or take a few bhp depending on the setting of the waste gate and thus maximum boost. A limited slip diff figured in the specification, sometimes running fully locked – shades of the 917. The suspension was by coil springs all round, so there were no torsion bars at all. At the front, 10.5-inch rims were retained, but those at the rear grew to 17 inches. Almost all external panels were glass-fiber, including the deep front spoiler. At the rear there was a huge spoiler, supported on two fin-like structures with the intercooler between them. Since the lip over the top edge of the rear window had been found to have a deleterious effect on air flow over the tail, the rear window was raised flush with the roof line.

The Turbo Carrera only raced for one season, in 1974. The most regular drivers were Herbert Müller and Gijs van Lennep, and their most outstanding result was a second at Le Mans where, if steering and gearbox problems had not intervened, they might have won. The same pair achieved another second at Watkins Glen, third at Spa, fifth at Monza, sixth at the 'Ring, and seventh at Paul Ricard. Not bad for a car that was, under the skin, basically a production machine.

Above: Le Mans 1978, and the famous – or infamous – low-line 'Moby Dick' 935.

Top: The 935's finest hour; the Kremer 935 K3 won Le Mans in 1979, driven by Klaus Ludwig and the American brothers Don and Bill Whittington.

leaving the World Championship of Sports Cars, effectively the old 3-liter Group 6 prototype formula, as the most important.

Porsche, therefore, attacked on three fronts in 1976, and the cars they used were the 934, the 935 and the 936. The names are significant, since they indicate that the base car was the 930, for Group 4, 5 and 6 (though the latter connection was a touch tenuous).

The 934, with the blown 3-liter engine, had an imaginary capacity of 4.2 liters when the equivalency factor came into play. To bring it up to the minimum weight it was barely stripped at all – even the electric windows were left in place. The 934 was obviously close to the standard product. The major difference between the standard 930 and the 934 came under the hood: the cooling fan lay horizontally, driven by belts and shafts and bevel gears. In addition there was a water-air intercooler, since an air-air device would not fit within the confines of the body as defined by the regulations. And Bosch K-Jetronic fuel injection was used for the first time on a Porsche racer. Thus equipped, the official output was 485bhp at 7000rpm, though another 100bhp could be squeezed out. There was a reinforcing bar between the MacPherson strut suspension towers, additional helper coil springs wrapped around the struts for fine tuning of the suspension, and BBS 16-inch wheels were standard.

About thirty 934s were made initially by Porsche, and they were all soon sold. Two names familiar in the Porsche story, Kremer and Loos, were among the customers, and Bob Wollek in the Kremer car and Toine Hezemans in the Loos car dominated the German GT classes in 1976. Buyers in America included Vasek Polak, usually described as 'irrepressible,' who bought five for George Follmer and Hurley Haywood to drive, Follmer winning the 1976 Trans-Am Championship in one, and Hezemans cleaned up the European Championship. Like so many Porsches before it, the 934 would have a long career on the tracks and you still see the occasional one today at smaller meetings.

Porsche's second string to their bow for 1976 was to become yet another of the most famous racing cars in the history of the sport, the incredible 935. With the 935, Porsche drew on their experience with the 2.14-liter Turbo Carrera. To keep below the effective 4-liter class, and, therefore, keep the weight down, a capacity of 2856cc was chosen: the official power output was 590bhp at 7900rpm, and the engine was similar to that of the 934, but with mechanical fuel injection.

The nose was filled with a vast fuel tank, surrounded by strengthening aluminum tubes. Titanium coil springs replaced the torsion bars all round, and the rear antiroll bar could be adjusted by the driver from within the cockpit. The brakes were developed from those of the 917. The whole car, of course, was lightened considerably, even if the entire body structure was standard – the floor

As an aside, the 2.14-liter engine carried on, but not in the Turbo Carrera. In 1975 it appeared in Reinhold Jöst's venerable 908/03; the car was a contender for World Championship honors but the works Alfas dominated. It did manage a second at Monza, though, and – with a normally aspirated 3-liter flat six – it finished fourth overall at Le Mans in what was generally a dismal race, hampered by fuel restrictions. That was also the first year for a long time that there had been no official works Porsche team at Le Mans since the intended changes to the regulations were postponed for a year, to 1976.

Categories in the new rules included Group 3, for Production Touring Cars, Group 4 for Limited Production Touring Cars, and Group 5 which would take in the World Championship of Makes, and the one on which Porsche placed a lot of hopes. This more or less encompassed Groups 1 to 4 but with considerable modification allowed, and a minimum weight based on a sliding scale depending on capacity, while the basic bodyshell, the major castings and their location, the general layout and the type of suspension had to be close to standard.

However, it began to look as if Porsche would be the only company contesting the Championship, and it might, therefore, be called off,

Right: The colorful paint job of this Hawaiian Tropic-sponsored 935 seemed to be lucky in 1979 – the car, driven by Rolf Stommelen, Dick Barbour and Paul Newman, came home second overall.

Below: A late development of the 935 was the Kremer brothers' effort in 1982.

pan came straight from the production line. So light was it, in fact, that ballast had to be added, but then it could be placed where it was most needed which was no bad thing. Most of the non-structural panels were made from a glass-fiber polyurethane sandwich, including the doors, engine cover, and the whole of the nose, taking in the front fenders and valance/spoiler.

The 935 featured a massive double-decker rear wing which was supported by a boxlike structure which also housed the bulky air-air intercooler. However, at one of the early races – Imola – the scrutineers objected to this set up since, according to the rules, the original engine cover should be able to be fitted to the rear of the 935: with the intercooler in place this was impossible. Porsche resorted to a water-air intercooler housed within the bodywork, but this was not a straightforward swap, and it took a little while to get it working.

After a couple of races, too, the front fenders were modified in a way that the rule-makers had most definitely not intended when they drew up the 'silhouette formula,' but which was quite within the letter of the law. The regulations stated that the fender shape was free, the intention being to allow additional width to cover racing tires without any unsightly, tacked-on, spats. Porsche took the regulations literally: the first 935s had the one-piece fender/spoiler unit based on the standard shape but they then chopped off the bulge formed by the headlamp and the top of the fender. This altered the whole look of the car but was important aerodynamically: it gave better penetration, more downforce at the front, and better side-wind sta-

Left: The lengthy tubular framework in the rear of the 936 was necessary to carry the equally lengthy tail (Le Mans, 1979).

bility. The headlamps were dropped down into a position in the front spoiler. The rule-makers did not like it but there was nothing they could do about it. It would also become wildly popular years later with the customizers, and even in 1985 Porsche would offer something similar on the road-going 930 Turbo Special Equipment.

While the 935 development program was under way in 1975, there was still some doubt about the viability of the 'silhouette formula': only Porsche seemed to be taking it seriously, while firms such as Renault and Alfa were pushing for a Sports Car Championship for Group 6 cars. The FIA dithered, as ever, and it looked as if Groups 5 and 6 would run together. Only Group 5 would count for a championship, but the chances were that the Group 6 cars would win overall. The importance of being seen to be first past the flag was not lost on Porsche.

Fuhrmann broke with his own philosophy, and made the decision to go for Group 6 as well. The go-ahead was given in September 1975, and the first car was built incredibly quickly, being tested in February 1976. As before, the new car, the 936, tended to be evolutionary, in the sense that Porsche had many of the right parts available: all that was really necessary was to make the right chassis and fit them to it. The most important of these

Below: 1979 was not a good year for the works 936s, in spite of Essex sponsorship. This is a rare shot of one in action at Silverstone before it had a big accident.

was obviously the engine and there, sitting in the parts bin, was the 2.14-liter turbocharged unit from 1974, ideal for the 3-liter capacity limit once the equivalency factor was taken into account. The transaxle and much of the suspension was taken almost directly from the 917, while the body shape drew on 917/30 experience. The all-new space frame was longer and lower than the 917/30's and departed slightly from previous practice in that the engine was mounted rigidly in it, thus imparting additional strength. When the 936 was announced, it was almost as big a surprise as the 917 had been some years earlier.

Porsche entered two 936/76s in 1976, sponsored by Martini, in the World Sports Car Championship. During secret testing before any racing was indulged in, the car was finished in matt black as a disguise, which fooled no one. However, Count Rossi, of sponsors Martini and Rossi, liked it, and for its first race at the 'Ring a 936 appeared in the same color but with Martini stripes added. However, it did not show up too well on the television cameras, particularly in the rain which accompanied the race, so from then on it was abandoned. In the race itself, in spite of the fact that the Renaults managed to take each other out, a stretched throttle cable relegated Rolf Stommelen in the car to fifth.

That Nürburgring race was the only one the 936 did not win that year. For Le Mans a huge air scoop was installed above and behind the driver's head, and a higher mounted wing took advantage of a minor change in the regulations. However, with the lower chassis, the driver sat much closer to assorted radiators with devastating results to his feet. This did not stop Ickx and van Lennep cantering home to a fairly easy win, in spite of a lengthy pit stop to replace a broken exhaust pipe. That year, 1976, 26 Porsches started at Le Mans, a 936 won overall, a 935 dominated Group 5, as did a 934 Group 4, while a Carrera took the IMSA category – not a bad record.

For 1977 there were a few changes to the rules for Group 5. To allow room under front-engined cars for turbocharging and exhaust systems, the floor was allowed to be raised to the level of the door sills: the bulkhead between engine and cockpit could be moved a few inches; and the 'body structure' was deemed to be that portion of the shell between front and rear cockpit bulkheads. Norbert Singer, the man in charge of the 935 program, was an expert at interpreting rules – witness the new nosepiece for the 1976 cars. So, for the 935/77, he used the new engine/cockpit bulkhead law to provide space for a larger intercooler. There were other changes too, to the suspension and engine, whch now featured twin, smaller, blowers for more rapid response. Small fins sprouted on the nose, cowling the mirrors, and the whole of the tail was redesigned with a completely new rear end covering the standard bodywork, taking full advantage of the rules governing

'aerodynamic aids.' Included in this was an additional perspex window which covered the original – the latter had to remain but could also be made from perspex.

Between the Martini-sponsored works cars and the private 935s, Porsche won every round of the World Championship of Makes in 1977. (They also won every round of the Trans-Am series, and seven out of 14 rounds of the IMSA Camel GT Championship). However, in the sub-2-liter class there was a battle going on between BMW and Ford, and the German media latched on to this, ignoring the over 2-liter class (which was, of course, in a hammer-lock by Porsche). Dr Fuhrmann did not like this one little bit, so he decided to join in.

Above: This 935 was only the second car to win Le Mans twice, in 1984 and 1985. This shot is from the latter year when the drivers were Ludwig, Barilla and 'John Winter.'

Below: By 1976 Porsche were regular Le Mans winners, and that year it was the turn of Jackie Ickx (yet again) and Gijs van Lennep.

Above: The 956 was
followed by the 962 –
this is the Skoal
Bandit-sponsored car
of John Fitzpatrick.

Right: It may not look
it, but buried beneath
that mass of
machinery in a 962 is
what could be called
a stock 911 engine.

His weapon was the 935/2. Taking advantage of
the 'body structure' rule, Singer removed the nose
and tail from a 911 shell, replacing the load-bear-
ing parts with frameworks of aluminum tubing.
The engine was a diminutive 1.4-liter turbocharged version of Porsche's faithful flat six, albeit
in nothing like its original state. With a tiny bore
and stroke the requisite capacity was achieved,
and the little engine gave 370bhp. Unfortunately
the preparation had been too hurried, and in its
first outing an overheated Jacky Ickx retired. It
was entered for one more race at Hockenheim,
and by this time it was sorted. Ickx won with ease.
Fuhrmann had made his point, that Porsche could
take on anyone, but also realized that the small-
capacity class was one in which Porsche did not
belong. Their production cars were all of greater
capacity. The 935/2 was withdrawn and never
raced again although a privately-entered 935 with
the 1.4-liter engine later appeared.

In 1977 the 936 only raced once, but, of course,
that was at Le Mans. The major modification was a
pair of KKK turbochargers on the 2.14-liter engine,
though there were a couple of detailed body alterations as well. Both cars suffered problems in
the race, the Ickx/Pescarolo car falling out with a
con rod through the side, and the Haywood/
Jürgen (son of Edgar) Barth car being delayed for
a long time with fuel-pump problems. When it got
going again Ickx transferred to it, and when the
Bell/Jabouille Renault expired on the Sunday
morning it took a lead it was never to lose. Mind
you, towards the end it was a mite fraught: a piston
holed. But such was the lead that the 936 stag-

Above: Porsche re-entered Formula 1 again in 1983 by supplying engines to McLaren, and promptly took the World Championship in 1984 and 1985. This is Prost at Estoril in 1985.

gered across the line on five cylinders still in front. Naturally a 935 driven by Claude Ballot-Lena and Peter Gregg took Group 5 and a Kremer 934 Group 4.

Singer's 'tweak of the week' for the 935 in 1978 was to take advantage, yet again, of the body regulations by removing the floor-to-sill level completely and replacing it with a tubular frame and glass-fiber floor, lowering the whole car by 3 inches. Learning from the 1.4-liter 'Baby,' the complete nose and tail were also replaced with tubes, covered by extended bodywork, which gave the car an odd hump-backed look and a nickname Moby Dick.

Right: Lauda at the British GP in 1984.

This car saw probably the first major alteration to the 911 engine. It looked as if the two-valve heads were getting close to their limit on both power output and reliability. Four valves was the obvious route to follow, and that meant one thing: water-cooled heads. Thus the new engine retained the 930 Turbo bottom end but with new water-cooled heads on top. The twin overhead camshafts per bank were operated by a chain of gears. One technical novelty was that the heads were electron-beam welded to the cylinders, thus eliminating any gaskets.

The new engine came with three possible capacities: 3211cc for Group 5, 2140cc for Group 6 and 2650cc for Indianapolis. However, Porsche misread the signals from the brickyard: the Americans were not going to have the Europeans coming over as they had done in the 1960s and trample all over them. They insisted on a boost rating too low to give the engine a chance, much to Porsche's annoyance, and amid much acrimony, the project was cancelled a month before the race. The Indy car sits in the Porsche Museum, unused to this day. The 3.2-liter unit was fitted into the 935/78 Moby Dick car. This gave a nominal capacity of 4.5 liters and hence a slight weight penalty but it also gave it a good top speed for Le Mans.

Moby Dick scored a runaway win at Silverstone in the 6 Hours race, prior to Le Mans, and looked a good bet for the Sarthe circuit (with 750bhp available, it recorded 222mph down the straight) but an apparently serious oil leak kept it down in eighth position. There were three other works cars at Le Mans in 1978, all 936/78s, with the mixture very much as before except that the 2.1-liter engines were fitted with the water-cooled heads. Two were new cars with droopy wings at the back, the third a 1977 car brought up to 1978 specification. All had their problems, and a Renault won with the 936s in second and third places.

For 1979, Porsche contracted out their works racing efforts, only entering two 936s for Le Mans – and even that was a last-minute decision. It looked as if Renault was dropping out of the sports-car game to concentrate on Grand Prix racing, but when they entered for Le Mans, Porsche had to do the same. The cars, running for this one race in Essex Petroleum colors, both fell out, but this was irrelevant since a Porsche won. This time, though, it was a Kremer 935 K3 in first place, driven by Klaus Ludwig and the Whittington brothers: in fact, they led from near enough midnight on Saturday to the end. The Dick Barbour 935 was second (its crew included the actor Paul

Below: The Joest Racing, New Man-sponsored 956 on its way to its first win at Le Mans in 1984 driven by Pescarolo and Ludwig.

Newman) and another Kremer 935 was third. The fourth-place car was a 934 which led the Group 4 category from start to finish.

The only works participation in 1980 was, as usual, at Le Mans – but not with 935s or 936s. The team that year consisted of three 924 Carrera GTPs, which, with 1.3 bar boost instead of the standard car's 0.7 bar, gave up to 320bhp. One car was driven by Lichtensteiner Jürgen Barth and Manfred Schurti, one by an American team (Peter Gregg and Al Holbert), and the third by a British team (Andy Rouse and Tony Dron). Since they had to run in the prototype category, a sixth by Barth/Schurti 12th by the Brits and 13th by the Americans was praiseworthy. The overall winner was a Rondeau, but in second place was the indomitable Jacky Ickx, partnering Reinhold Jöst (or Joest as it is often spelled) in a replica 936/77 which Jöst had built in his own workshops.

The 3-liter limit for Group 6 was abolished in 1981, so Porsche upped the capacity of the 936 by fitting it with the 2560cc engine that should have gone in the Indy car. Detuned to run on pump fuel, and with low boost for longer life, it still gave some 600bhp. Two works 936s appeared at the start, one was delayed by assorted faults during the race, but the Ickx/Bell car led from start to finish without any major problems, taking the chequered flag four laps ahead of the second-place Rondeau and giving Jacky his fifth victory at Le Mans. Other cars to race included the 924 Carrera in the GTP (GT Prototype) class but fitted with the Porsche-designed four from the 944. With twin

camshafts, four valves per cylinder, and a turbocharger, it gave a sound 450bhp, and finished a healthy seventh overall. There was also, believe it or not, a 917 in the race: it was entered by Erwin Kremer's team and was a brand-new car, not one of the old cars resurrected. The ex-Rodriguez Gulf car was borrowed so that an exact copy could be constructed, and a 4.9-liter engine was installed. However, it was slow and did not make it past the eighth hour. Jöst reappeared with his replica 936, too.

And so to 1982, for which FISA introduced a new category in the World Endurance Championship (WEC), Group C. This was the only pure track-racing category in the newly revised Appendix J, Groups A, B and N being for production cars, intended for dual usage in both racing and rallying. Group C replaced both Group 5 and 6, and was essentially a fuel-economy formula. Any engine could be used provided it came from a manufacturer who had homologated cars in either Group A or B. Emphasis was placed on efficiency, however, by restricting the fuel available to each car, and the tankage to 100 liters. It also attempted to restrict any ground effects by insisting on a plate, 39 inches by 31 inches, underneath the cars, below which no part of the bodywork could protrude. However, FISA found itself struggling for fixtures, particularly in America, where the leading road-racing organization, IMSA, declined to adopt Group C as its premier class for sound local reasons. Thus the World Endurance Championship of Makes was run over only five events,

Below: The Belga-sponsored Joest Racing 956 at the Nürburgring in 1982.

the Championship for Drivers over eight. Porsche jumped at the formula – they had been making excellent, at times spectacular, progress at improving their production-car economy, and this was a way of showing the direction in which they felt motor racing should develop.

For the new formula, Porsche designed what was, for them, a radically new car. For a start, it was the first racing Porsche to feature a monocoque chassis. It also introduced ground effect. The engine was the 2.6-liter Indy unit, worked over in the interests of better economy, but still giving about 620bhp, depending on how much boost was run. There was a new five-speed Porsche transmission, the coupé bodywork was honed in the wind tunnel, and, of course, it was subjected to the company's awesome pre-race test-development program at Weissach before making its debut at the Silverstone 6 Hours. In that first race it was slowed to preserve fuel and finish – even Porsche sometimes get their sums wrong.

Nevertheless, three 956s were entered for Le Mans in 1982, backed up by two more Group C cars: one was a space-frame device, powered by the 2.1-liter engine, from Reinhold Jöst, the other an all-new car from Kremer, the K5. This used a 2.8-liter 935 engine but in the Kremer's own space-frame chassis.

The result is now history. For this, the 50th anniversary of the 24-hour race on the Sarthe circuit, Jacky Ickx, partnered by Derek Bell, won his sixth victory, and the 956s demolished all opposition, rolling across the line in 1-2-3 formation, Mass and Schuppan second and Haywood and Holbert third. Two 935s followed them home, giving Porsche one of their best years ever.

With three outright wins, Porsche took the 1982 Make's Championship, and Ickx the Driver's, though it was a closer run thing than the statistics indicate, for Ford-Rondeau could have taken the Makes, and Riccardo Patrese or Michael Alboreto the Drivers.

For 1983, FISA retained the basic format of Group C for the WEC in its second season: a free-engine formula with practical limitations on power output imposed by fuel restrictions. They also retained Group B and were rewarded with far stronger participation than before, albeit with re-homologated machinery. Alongside the Makes Championship there was the Drivers World Championship and a new one, the European Endurance Championship of Drivers. Unfortunately there was still the FISA/IMSA split, in effect turning what should have been one worldwide series into two, lesser (but still important) series.

The main opposition to the Porsches came from Lancia – and the privateers who had purchased 12 customer versions of the 956 on offer. The works 956-83s, with Rothmans backing, were basically the 1982 cars updated, with lighter chassis, suspension revisions, various high-downforce nose sections, and, above all, the electronic-engine-management system. After a shock defeat at the first round at Monza by the Jöst Racing customer 956, Porsche instigated a short crash program to improve fuel consumption, which proved

crushingly effective, the Rothmans-Porsches winning six other rounds from then on. At Le Mans, three irregular works drivers, Al Holbert, Vern Schuppan and Hurley Haywood, carried off the victory – and what a race it was! During the last stint, the hapless Holbert had to struggle with a seriously overheating engine, which finally lost all its water with a lap to go. Perhaps the air cooling of the block helped, but somehow the unit kept going over the last 8½ miles and enabled Al, on the edge of hysteria, to crawl across the line, first in an extraordinary race in which 956s filled nine of the top ten places, the Ickx/Bell Rothmans car in second place.

At the end of the year Porsche had won the Makes Championship by 100 points to Lancia's 32, Ickx (with Bell a close second) the Drivers Championship, and Bob Wollek the European Drivers Championship in the Jöst Racing cars. Porsche 930s took the Group B Championship as well. Porsche built 12 customer 956s, 11 of which were sold and raced during the season, which were basically 1982-specification cars with all-mechanical engine controls and a lower compression ratio. Jöst won at Monza and Mugello and John Fitzpatrick Racing at Brands Hatch.

The start of the 1984 season saw FISA drop a bombshell with a fundamental rule change, designed, yet again, to amalgamate the WEC and the IMSA GTP Championships. In the furore that followed, Porsche angrily withdrew the works cars from Le Mans, but such was the domination of the 956s in this series that the result was never seriously in doubt, in spite of the threat from Lancia yet again. The WEC events numbered 11, and the European series was scrapped so that there were just two world championships, for Makes and Drivers.

Over the winter of 1983/84, Helmuth Bott's research and development division at Weissach had been at full stretch to meet the demand for customer cars, 956s for Group C and 962s for the IMSA series. Thus Peter Falk, the competitions director, had to rely on the 1983 cars, the only technical development being more work with Bosch on the engine management systems and the testing of an ingenious, electronically controlled, twin-clutch transmission designed for full-throttle gear changes.

The works Rothmans-Porsches, nevertheless, made a perfect start to the season, with Bellof and Bell winning at Monza. Bellof, in fact, turned out to

Below: Rear suspension and transmission of a 956 – note high-mounted, angled rear springs.

be the sensation of the season, and, thanks to a seat in the winning car on no fewer than six occasions (five times at the wheel of a Rothmans car, once in the private Brun car), he walked away with the Drivers Championship, the Rothmans-Porsches taking the Makes Championship by winning seven of the races in the series.

With no works cars at Le Mans, Porsche were represented by all the major privateers such as Jöst, GTI/Canon, Brun, Fitzpatrick and Kremer. In contrast to the works, these teams became very active in the development of the 956s, several of them coming up with their own aerodynamic packages (GTI and Jöst successfully), and GTI constructed its own honeycomb-chassis version of the car. Jöst and Fitzpatrick came to reject the inflexibility of the pre-programmed Bosch Motronic customer engine, and on occasion raced with mechanically controlled units (in fact, the privateers' season began with an expensive sequence of 16 engine failures caused by an ignition-programming fault).

Jöst received their new 956 just before Le Mans, and it qualified fourth fastest. The first few hours were a debacle, the car at one point being dead last. However, by the dint of consistently fast driving, Henri Pescarolo and Klaus Ludwig took

Above: A familiar sight in 1984 and 1985 – the Rothmans' Porsches at the head of the field, in this case the Norisring in 1983. The only interloper in the following string of cars is a Lancia.

Left: Long-time Porsche driver John Fitzpatrick.

advantage of the attrition rate, moved into the top ten in the sixth hour, and at 7.10 a.m. on Sunday morning took the lead, never to relinquish it. It was a famous victory, Pescarolo's fourth and Ludwig's second. Porsche 956s filled eight of the top-ten positions at the end, too.

To cover themselves just in case the IMSA GTP rules were adopted by FISA – and to sell cars and keep in the forefront of sports-car racing in America – Porsche developed a new model for 1984, the 962. Although an offshoot of the all-conquering 956, it was not the same car: a 12cm longer wheelbase (the GTP rules required the driver's feet to be behind the front suspension) meant a new monocoque, different nose, different tail, different fuel cell and a radically altered engine bay. The standard engine was the 2.85 liter, two-valve, single-plug, single-turbo device. The prototype debuted at Daytona in February in the hands of Michael and Mario Andretti, where it started from pole but failed with transmission problems. From then on Derek Bell and Al Holbert campaigned a 962 and, although they won five races before the end of the year, they could not catch the series winners Randy Lanier and Bill Whittington in a March-Chevrolet.

The season in 1985 in the WEC rounds was at first dominated by the 15 percent reduction in the fuel allowance, many of the teams simply struggling to finish without running out. However, developments by Bosch, and the use of 'high aromatic' fuels by some teams, soon overcame the prob-

lems. For the first round at Mugello, the works fielded a pair of new 962C cars and a 956 as a spare: the 962Cs were fitted with 2.6-liter power plants equipped with the latest Bosch Motronic gadgetry. For this year the 962C has taken over from the 956 as the car to have, Brun and Kremer entering them as well at Mugello. In fact, both of these cars led at one point but ran short of fuel and had to crawl over the line, overhauled by Mass/Ickx in the factory car, who had disciplined themselves to a correct race strategy. Nevertheless, there were four 962Cs in the first four positions at the end. The next round at Monza was stopped when a tree fell on the circuit. At the time the Kremer 962 driven by Manfred Winkelhock and Marc Surer was in the lead, so it was declared the winner ahead of Stuck and Bell in a 956, their 962 having been burned to a blob in a fire in practice. At Silverstone a couple of weeks later the Rothmans-Porsches were back in their accustomed positions, Ickx and Mass in the 962 winning by a lap from Bell and Stuck in their hybrid car, a 956 with a 962 rear end, a result of the fire at Monza. And so to Le Mans, where there was a real turnup for the books: the Jöst team won overall, using the very same 956B that had won the year before. It was not only the fastest throughout the weekend, but also the most fuel-efficient of the C1 cars, a fact that perplexed every other Porsche team and ultimately defeated them. In second place was another 956, the Canon entry driven by Jonathan Palmer and James Weaver. The first of the works

Above: The 1982 Rothmans' Porsche 956. Three such cars gave Porsche a 1-2-3 finish at Le Mans that year.

Below: The Joest 956 at Silverstone in 1982.

cars, a 962C driven by Bell and Stuck, was in third, another with Ickx and Mass behind the wheel in tenth. To rub salt into the works wounds, the winning car had led from the third hour.

Following Le Mans, Bell and Stuck (BEST in pit signals) won at Hockenheim, but it was a dramatic race. While the Mass/Ickx (MIX on pit signals) was being refuelled, there was a blow-back to a tank on top of the pits and an instant fire in which Norbert Singer was seriously burned. Disaster

again struck at Mosport when, in an inexplicable accident, the popular German driver of the Kremer 962C, Manfred Winkelhock, was killed. Possibly the most tragic moment, though, came at Spa when the immensely talented Stefan Bellof, in a Brun 956, tangled with Jacky Ickx at Eau Rouge and was killed when his car hurtled into the barrier. At the end of the season the Factory Rothmans-Porsche team won the new World Endurance Championship of Teams (changed from

Makes), with BEST sharing the driver's title, but 1985 was not a vintage year. There was some good racing but the deaths of Bellof and Winkelhock, and the fires at Hockenheim, made it a year to forget.

One driver whose name, along with that of Jacky Ickx, is synonymous with Porsche is Derek Bell, and in an interview in 1984 he gave his views on the cars he has driven:

First of all, Porsche are, simply, the most professional team I've ever worked with: they are very intense about their racing. One thing that's stuck in my mind is that I've never heard any of the engineers raise his voice to a mechanic. There's always an air of calm, a lack of panic in the Porsche pits.

The first Porsche I ever drove was the 917, and it was and is to me the greatest ever. It was a magnificent car to drive, it had a personality of its own. I went back to one at an historic race meeting in 1983 and it was just like a dream, like rekindling an old romance. It has far more usable power than something like a 956.

The 917 was followed by the 935. I looked forward so much to driving it, but was terribly disappointed! It was very brutal, especially in the early days when it only had the single turbo – you

had to wait for the power to come on. When you look at it, with the engine stuck out the back, it's a very unsophisticated car. To have 750bhp or whatever is great, but not in the 935. You had to be very hard with it, attack it, until you got to know it (it took Jacky a whole winter to master it when it first came out). I prefer a little more finesse when I'm racing. Mind you, it was very reliable and, of course, perfect for private owners because of this, but then there was no opposition to it in Group 5, which is what effectively killed that category and the car with it – it was a sheer case of overkill. The Kremer K3s weren't that bad, but I never enjoyed the 935 very much.

I only drove a 936 once, at Le Mans in 1981, when, of course, Jacky and I won. In spite of that, I regard it as a lovely car, a classic. It was so light, so delicate. At first the brakes were bloody awful, but then Porsche found the problem and cured it – they always do. The Indy engine gave all its power at the top end, and we only had a four-speed box, so there were times – like in the Porsche curves – when you tended to be in the wrong gear, but that was about the only flaw. It was never really developed, though – they just kept changing the engine, didn't they?

I'll always remember the last few laps of that

race. I knew I'd never race it again, so I really gave it stick (away from the pits, of course!) and it was absolutely marvellous: I just sat back and enjoyed it. A lovely car, a beautiful 24-hour experience. It was similar to the 917 in that respect, a nice easy car to drive.

Coming to the 956, I remember when Bott first told me about it. He looked at me and said, 'We've never had ground effect before, nor a monocoque.' Pause. 'But we've never been wrong before!' and, of course, he was right. With ground effect it was, naturally, very quick, but the springing was ultra-stiff and I didn't take to that at all – I thought it would break either the car or driver over a 24-hour period! Horrible, just horrible. However, you get used to ground effect very quickly – I learnt all about it at Weissach.

The 956 doesn't have much character, though, it's just a beautifully efficient machine, easy to drive, with no bad habits, although it can be a bit tricky on the limit.

While Porsche has spent the last 25 years dominating the sports-racing world, the 911 has emerged yet again as a winner in a sphere so totally different as to be mind-boggling: the Paris-Dakar Rally. This sort of event seems to hold a fascination for Porsche: back in the early 1970s they made serious attempts to win the gruelling, car-breaking East African Safari rally. In 1971 they entered a three-car team of 2.2-liter 911Ss, two of which fell out with suspension damage. The third, driven by Zasada, had little trouble until an engine misfired not far from the finish, when it was in with a chance for a win, and dropped back to fifth. Porsche tried again in 1973, with Carrera RSs, but again suspension damage, compounded by transmission problems, forced them out. They returned once more, in 1974, with just one car, a 2.7 Carrera RS, for Bjorn Waldegaard. This time the suspension and transmission lasted but a half-shaft broke. Waldegaard was happy with second, under the circumstances. They tried yet again, in 1978, with an impressive team which included Waldegaard and Vic Preston Jnr. In spite of meticulous preparations, and some 10 tons of spares (including the cars), Waldegaard broke a rear suspension arm and Preston a half-shaft, enough to put Waldegaard into fourth place and Preston into second – again.

Porsche's involvement with the Paris-Dakar came about through the indomitable Jacky Ickx, who seems to have a thoroughly masochistic streak in him. Not being content to make a 24-hour race his own (Le Mans), he entered the 1983 event in a 911 and won. So enthused was he with the event that the next year, 1984, there was a Team Jacky Ickx, ostensibly private but with Rothmans' sponsorship and considerable help from Porsche including two trucks and a third Porsche driven by factory mechanics. The cars were four-wheel-drive 911SCs, and previous winner René Metge had a relatively trouble-free run to the winner's rostrum. Ickx, in fact, was fastest over seven stages to Metge's one, but suffered mechanical delays which dropped him to sixth at the finish. In fact, the factory mechanics, Roland Kussmaul and Eric Lerner, won two stages in the back-up car.

The team was back again in 1985, this time with cars that were externally similar to the 959 Group B machine, but only the bodyshell and variable four-wheel-drive system came from the 959. The engine was a trusty 225bhp unblown flat six, and the team consisted of Ickx, Metge, and Jochen Mass. Alas, this time all three retired, but at least Porsche have now considerable experience in rallying with four-wheel-drive. What chance a 959 in there with the Peugeots, Audis, Fords, Lancias and Metros next year?

But back, now, in time to 1983, to the Geneva Show in March. Another Porsche bombshell: a new engine – for Grand Prix racing. Not since 1962 had a Porsche engine been seen on an F1 grid, and that had been a traumatic experience. Time and again Porsche said they were not interested in F1, their forte was endurance sports-car racing where they ruled the roost and that they would leave the single seaters to the specialists. However, they did not say they would not design and make an engine for someone else, using their renowned research and development facilities just as they did for SEAT, for example. And that is just what happened.

In the early 1980s it was becoming obvious that the previously all-conquering Cosworth V8 was being overtaken by events, notably turbocharged engines. Although limited to half the capacity of a naturally aspirated engine, developments in turbochargers for small-capacity petrol engines had come a long way, and peak power was being limited by what mechanical stress the engine could take, and what peak boost the blower could give. Power characteristics, with everything at the top end, were not popular but once drivers learned how to control a turbo engine they took

Below: Porsche made the infamous Paris-Dakar rally almost entirely their own, Ickx winning it in 1983 with a two-wheel-drive 911 and Metge in 1984 in this four-wheel-drive version.

off, literally and metaphorically. Renault was first on the scene, followed by Ferrari. BMW supplied engines to Brabham, and Alfa Romeo and Toleman had turbocharged engines too.

McLaren's Ron Dennis went to Stuttgart and spoke to the Porsche hierarchy. Would they, he asked, be willing to tackle an F1 engine program? Yes, they said, if he could find the financial backing – it had to be on a purely commercial basis. Dennis found the backing in the Arabian Ojieh's family concern, *Techniques d'Avant Garde*, or TAG for short. They sponsored the Williams team, and when Dennis approached them they agreed to form a joint company, TAG Turbo engines, which certainly would put money into the F1 engine project.

Porsche's design was classically simple and elegant. It was an 80 deg V6 of 1499cc, with four valves per cylinder, four overhead camshafts, alloy heads and magnesium alloy block, titanium con rods, forged steel pistons and crankshaft, and

two KKK turbochargers feeding the engine via water-air intercoolers. At 150 kg it was light (30 kg less than the BMW), and gave an official 650bhp, with peak power being developed between 10,000 and 11,500rpm. Above all, though, it featured the Bosch Motronic engine management system, something that Porsche and Bosch had been working on for the sports-car racers, where fuel restrictions required engines to run efficiently, not just give as much power as possible. There were threatened restrictions in F1 as well, in an attempt to reduce the escalating power outputs. Porsche realized that there would be some form of performance limitation, so right from the beginning they looked for a balance between out-and-out power and good fuel consumption.

With McLaren, Porsche found a company that could match them when it came to meticulous preparation, good design, and general all-round competence. In addition they had superb drivers, with Niki Lauda and John Watson in 1983, and

Below: Just occasionally Porsche produce some strange color schemes, but few could have been stranger or more menacing than the matt black of the first 936. However, it didn't show up well on television so was rapidly dropped.

Lauda again and Alain Prost in 1984. The engine is only one part of winning, but it's a vital part.

The results are now history. In 1983 the McLaren-TAGs made a slow start as various maladies were sorted out, but in 1984 they swept the board in a stunning display of almost complete mastery. Together Lauda and Prost won 12 out of 16 Grands Prix in a season where they were not only demonstrably faster than almost anyone else except Nelson Piquet in the fragile Brabham, but that they were also the most frugal. Others had to slow, simply to conserve fuel: the McLarens didn't. Allied to the Porsche-TAG engines output and economy was the legendary Porsche reliability. It was a winning combination.

It would have been difficult, almost impossible, to repeat the stunning 1984 results in 1985, and sure enough matters did not go McLaren-TAG's way all the time. Ferrari fought back early in the year, but faded. At Lotus, Ayrton Senna revitalized the team and was arguably the fastest driver around but to win you need to finish: Lotus did so only three times at the front. A stronger challenge came from Williams and in particular from the dazzling Keke Rosberg – but they too only scored

four wins, two by Nigel Mansell. But it was McLaren, with six wins, five by the cool Alain Prost, which had scored most points at the end of the season. Prost and McLaren were the champions. What makes this result all the more creditable is the fact that the TAG-Porsche engine is acknowledged to be down on power compared to the Renaults, Hondas and BMWs that power the other cars: once again it was the Porsche forte, that combination of power with reliability (and, this season, economy) that won through in the end, and after all it's winning that counts.

The problem with writing a history of Porsche is that you are aiming at a moving target. There can be no doubt that by the time you read this, Porsche will yet again have added significantly to the history books.

There are constants, though. Performance is obviously one. Then there are quality standards second to none. Engineering in its highest form. Continuity and experience. It can perhaps best be summed up in one word: excellence.

Otherwise why would people go out and buy those bumper stickers that say 'My Other Car's A Porsche'?

Above: Porsche's current weapon in the sportscar racing field is the 962, which seems destined to be as famous as the 550, 718, 904, 906, 907, 908, 910, 917, 936 – and 956, of course. . . .

Overleaf: The team, 1985. . . .

INDEX

Page numbers in italics refer to illustrations

Author's Acknowledgments

The author would like to extend especial
thanks to all those who helped so enormously in
the production of this book, in particular the
photographic studio at Porsche in Stuttgart and
Jeremy Snook of Porsche GB. In addition his
two Editors, Quentin Spurring of *Autosport* and
Mark Hughes of *Classic and Sportscar*, who
ploughed their way through the typed words,
and his photographic colleagues – Mick Walsh,
Jeff Bloxham, Andrew Yeadon, Mike Valente,
Mel Dew and Paul Debois for proving that
pictures speak a thousand words . . .

Publisher's Acknowledgments

The publisher would like to thank Richard
Garratt the designer, Wendy Sacks who did
the picture research and Ron Watson who
compiled the index. Special thanks to Porsche
Cars (Great Britain) Ltd and Porsche Cars,
Stuttgart, West Germany for their generous
help in supplying photographs, as well as to the
agencies and individuals listed below:

Archive Mathe: page 125(top)
Aston Publications: page 115(bottom)
Jeff Bloxham: page 162-3, 166-7, 170(both),
171(top), 174(top)
Neill Bruce Photographic: pages 29(both), 30-1,
31(top), 54-5, 56, 58(top), 66(bottom), 81(top)
Neill Bruce/Nigel Dawes Collection: pages
93(inset), 99(top)
Neill Bruce/Midland Motor Museum,
Bridgnorth: pages 86, 87(top), 143(both)
Chris Harvey: pages 6-7, 64, 66(top),
99(bottom), 100, 110(bottom), 111, 161(top),
165(bottom), 175(both), 176(bottom)
Haymarket Publishing/Autocar: pages 94-5, 96
Haymarket Publishing/Autosport: pages
33(both), 34(top), 37(top), 39(top), 43, 48,
58(bottom), 83(top), 107(top), 117(top), 118-19,
120, 121, 123(top), 124, 128, 129(top),

133(bottom), 134(top), 135(top), 137,
141(bottom), 144(bottom), 150, 151(top), 152-3,
155(top and bottom right), 158(top),
161(bottom), 168-9, 169(top), 171(bottom) 172-
3(both), 174(bottom), 176(top), 180, 186
Haymarket Publishing/Classic and Sportscar:
pages 2-3, 4-5, 32(bottom), 49(bottom), 80,
81(bottom), 82, 154(bottom), 155(bottom left)
Haymarket Publishing/What Car?: page 91
LAT Photographic: page 146(bottom)
Günther Molter: pages 34(bottom), 116(top)
National Motor Museum, Beaulieu: pages 19,
26-7, 27(top), 28(top), 35(bottom), 36-7, 42,
49(top), 57(top), 67(bottom), 71, 98, 112(top),
113, 136, 149(top), 164
Doug Nye: page 157(bottom)
Porsche Cars: pages 8, 9(top left and top right),
11(both), 12(both), 14, 15, 16(bottom), 17, 20-1
(all 3), 22(both), 23, 34(center), 35(top), 38-9,
39(bottom), 40-1, 44-5(both), 46-7, 50-1, 52-3(all
4), 57(bottom), 59(both), 60-1, 67(top), 68, 73,
76-7, 78-9, 87(bottom), 92, 114, 115(top),
122(top), 122-3, 125(bottom), 126, 127(inset),
132(bottom), 138(top), 146(top), 147(bottom),
148-9, 154(top), 156(both), 160(both),
177(bottom), 178-9, 181(bottom), 182, 183(both),
184, 187, 188-9
Quadrant Picture Library/Autocar: pages
30(top), 31(bottom right), 65(top), 88-9, 116-17,
127(main pic), 158-9
Quadrant Picture Library/Motor: page 97
Quadrant Picture Library/Thoroughbred and
Classic Cars: pages 24-5, 130-1
Nigel Snowdon: pages 145, 147(top),
151(bottom)
TPS/CLI: pages 1, 32(top), 62-3(all 3),
65(bottom), 90-1, 93(main pic), 101, 132-3, 134-5
TPS/Keystone: page 18
Volkswagen/Audi: pages 13, 16(top)
Mick Walsh: pages 9(bottom), 10, 72-3, 102-3,
108-9, 110(top), 112(bottom), 129(bottom), 140
Nicky Wright: pages 26(top), 28(bottom), 69,
70, 74-5, 77(bottom), 83(bottom), 84-5, 88(inset),
95(both), 104, 105(both), 106, 107(bottom), 138
(bottom), 138-9, 141(top & center), 142, 144(top)